TO MY DARLING HUSBAND

GARY ROY

AND OUR

PRECIOUS SON

JOSHUA

Table of Contents

Introduction to African Folklore Embroidery

I cannot remember a time when my mother was not stitching, sewing or baking and my father did not have a hammer in his hand building, making or doing. I grew up in Cape Town, South Africa, with no television till the age of ten. My parents and grandparents encouraged in their children a love for creating with their hands. My mother sewed most of our clothes, my grandmother was a seamstress and milliner, and my father made our toys, including slides, puzzles, tree houses, educational toys, book shelves and much more, out of wood.

We were encouraged to create, make and take pride in work created with our hands. With aunts and cousins who lived next door there was always someone coming over for a cup of tea, a chat and some stitching. My grandfather had more hobbies and crafts than I can list, and promoted in us an active desire to learn something new every day.

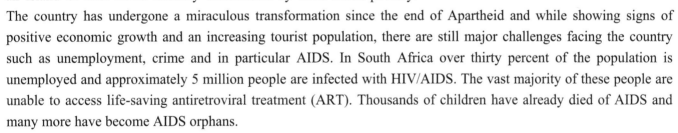

Like most African traditions that are passed down from mother to daughter, father to son, I learnt African Folklore Embroidery from my mother. Since I have a son, I have passed this art form on to him, and he has in turn taught his friends and classmates.

My parents and grandmother of 95 still live in Cape Town and both my husband and I have close family living in Johannesburg and Durban. So going back to Africa to spend time with family and friends, visit with tribes and experience African wildlife, traditions and customs on a continuous basis is an integral part of our lives.

South Africa while beautiful is a country of contradictions. It is an island of first-world industry surrounded by third-world poverty. The country has undergone a miraculous transformation since the end of Apartheid and while showing signs of positive economic growth and an increasing tourist population, there are still major challenges facing the country such as unemployment, crime and in particular AIDS. In South Africa over thirty percent of the population is unemployed and approximately 5 million people are infected with HIV/AIDS. The vast majority of these people are unable to access life-saving antiretroviral treatment (ART). Thousands of children have already died of AIDS and many more have become AIDS orphans.

Before coming to live in America, my work in South Africa involved undertaking research into different communities and villages, assessing their needs, wants and aspirations and communicating those needs to other groups. When Apartheid ended and Nelson Mandela became president of South Africa, bringing democracy, peace, hope and freedom to millions of people, there was a desire amongst various groups to gain some sort of understanding of each other. In the past ten years, South Africa's different cultures have come together to create the "rainbow nation." South Africa is a country diverse in cultures and traditions.

When I lived in South Africa, I had the opportunity to lecture on research at universities and while lecturing students I learnt so much about their cultures and communities, along with terms of respect and endearment appropriate in various tribal cultures.

Four years into our married life, my husband, Gary, and I decided to combine a work and leisure vacation in the United States. I was giving a lecture at a conference on investment opportunities in South Africa, and my husband was visiting his brother in Cleveland. We planned on meeting up at family in Los Angeles. Within days of our arrival in Los Angeles, my husband—an accountant—had been offered a position. He had always wanted to attain international financial experience and we felt that this was an exciting opportunity in his career.

I continued being involved and working in research, this time conducting primary and secondary analysis in

US sectors and industries, but I missed and felt a void between the country and culture I had left behind and the passion I had experienced for the community research in which I used to be involved.

A year after arriving in America our son, Joshua, was born—the happiest day of our lives. While I continued to work in research, the excitement I had once felt for writing reports, analyzing data and corporate deadlines was just not there. I wanted to be home every day to take my son to school, pick him up, and spend time together in the afternoons.

When my son was nearly four years old and I was recovering from both the physical and emotional impact of fertility treatments and several miscarriages, my mom came to visit me from South Africa and told me I needed to do "something with my hands." She placed the African Folklore Embroidery design into my hands and for the next hour she and I sat stitching side by side. It felt so relaxing and so soothing, I could not remember the last time I had experienced this feeling, this relaxed and at peace. It had something to do with the rhythmical and repetitive motion and I just did not want to put it down.

I started taking the African Folklore Embroidery with me wherever I went, folding the designs up in my purse and taking it out whenever I was waiting at the doctor's office, at the park with my son, on play dates, on

airplane trips, and every time I did this, complete strangers would come up to me, admire my work, ask me what I was doing, and inquire how they could learn to do African Folklore Embroidery and where they could buy a kit design. Every time I interacted with these people and someone wanted to learn how to do the African Folklore Embroidery it allowed me an opportunity to talk about my country of birth and answer questions, and I was excited to share this information with people. I found the interest in South Africa and African Folklore Embroidery, and the desire to learn more about this country, refreshing and inspiring. Friends would invite a group of friends to their house and ask me to come and show their friends how to do the African Folklore Embroidery; one friend told another and then someone suggested I should try doing a quilting trade show. Slowly the process began and my new passion started to grow into a small business.

I realized just how much I enjoyed teaching and showing people how to do the stitches and loved the fact that since the designs and threads were from South Africa, this allowed me to maintain a connection to the country of my birth. From there people started asking if I could teach African Folklore Embroidery at schools, camps, museums, and thereafter I started receiving invitations to lecture and conduct workshops at quilting guilds and quilt and craft shows across the country. People were not only interested in learning an ethnic and multicultural needle art; they were interested in expanding their horizons and learning about other cultures and communities.

I realized that however much I enjoyed doing the embroidery myself and showing others how to do it, there was a larger mission at stake—an opportunity to build a bridge between the country of my birth and my adopted country. I recognized that the lectures were an opportunity to not only teach a new craft but also to educate and expose Americans from all backgrounds to information about life in South Africa, and some of the fascinating customs and traditions of many of the tribes. I also realized that if in some small way this could help address the most serious issues facing South Africa— unemployment and AIDS—and I could share my passion and enthusiasm for African Folklore Embroidery, I would be delighted.

With South Africa's thirty percent unemployment rate, I have always believed that the more products that can be purchased from countries suffering high unemployment, the greater the stimulus in creating jobs and income for people in that country. With income generation comes self-esteem.

AIDS in South Africa and the rest of Africa is an everyday reality. Mothers in Africa battle their own HIV infection and devote themselves to the care of their HIV-infected children. While HIV/AIDS is incurable, children can live with AIDS for many years with the proper medication and care. Kidzpositive, an AIDS charity close to my heart at Groote Schuur Hospital in Cape Town, allows for mothers to receive raw materials to produce beadwork.

They are trained to make beaded items and sell these items as a means of income and support. These moms do not want handouts; they want to be able to say this week they have orders for their beaded items, thereby enabling money to be directly distributed to the mothers and their children who need it most. The more orders these moms get for their beaded products, the more they can provide for their families and the greater their self-esteem.

One way in which African Folklore Embroidery has made a contribution is by placing orders for hand beaded items from Kidzpositive. For every book purchased we will be placing an order and you, the readers, will receive your own hand-beaded pen from Kidzpositive, South Africa. Every visit back to South Africa involves time spent at Groote Schuur Hospital with the moms and children from Kidzpositive. They recently established a school, so taking back school supplies and some of the items on their wish list has become a priority. My mom's quilting group in South Africa makes quilts so that each child with HIV will receive their own quilt to take home.

You can learn more about Kidzpositive at www.kidzpositive.org. Another AIDS organization doing incredible work in South Africa, and with whom we are affiliated, is Starfish Charity. They provide food and school uniforms to HIV-infected children whose parents have died from AIDS. www.starfishcharity.org

Since it takes more than twenty hours to travel from America to South Africa, most people will never have the opportunity to experience Africa, the joy of seeing animals up close on a safari, or be exposed to cultural traditions and customs so different from their own. However, I hope this visual safari through African Folklore Embroidery and the teaching of the various stitches and techniques, interweaved with information about various tribes and their customs and traditions, along with African wildlife, will give you a small taste of Africa, its rich beauty and culture.

As interest in African Folklore Embroidery grew and the request for lectures and workshops on both a national and international basis increased, I developed the **African Folklore Embroidery Educator Program**, which allows through training, passionate and creative people to teach others about life in South Africa through African Folklore Embroidery.

After teaching over 6,000 adults and children the art of African Folklore Embroidery in the past four years, the questions started coming: "Where is the book?" And so, reader, what you have in front of you is a small piece of me, a taste of South Africa and the stitches, techniques and embellishment tools to complete an African Folklore Embroidery design.

Interspersed while viewing some of the completed designs you will see the various techniques and colors that have been used, and learn about African tribal life, wildlife and safaris, as well as some less explored areas of South Africa, its bird life, marine life and of course flora and fauna. I have also included some pictures of designs completed by some very talented women, and to end off some of my mom's South African recipes. I have also listed some of my favorite places to visit while in South Africa and where you can see some of the things I speak about in this book.

So sit back, relax and enjoy this visual African safari.

On Safari with African Folklore Embroidery

Welcome to the colorful and creative world of African Folklore. I am excited to have you aboard the safari. Have you got your camera and binoculars? Most people will not get the chance to visit or explore Africa, and those that do will need to go on a more than twenty-hour plane ride to do so. (Well worth it, but pretty long). This book brings Africa to you and allows you to get a small taste of Africa, its beautiful, diverse and vast cultures and traditions all through African Folklore Embroidery, a multi cultural visual fiber and bead art..

One of the main reasons people visit Africa is to go on safari and see the vast array of wild animals in their natural environment, free of cages and restrictions. Like any journey, our safari through African Folklore Embroidery is subject to a few rules, so before we begin our visual safari, let's go through these rules:

- RULE #1 - Whatever color you choose to stitch is the right color—there is no wrong color; if you wish to stitch your giraffes pink or your sun blue—go for it!

- RULE #2 - Your stitches do **not** need to be perfect—there are no needle art police who are going to come and inspect your work! Life is not perfect! You will be pleasantly surprised how stunning your design will look with imperfections.

- RULE #3 - The needles are only to be used for stitching, No poking anyone or sewing yourself! (Obvious, but worth mentioning). <u>Always secure or "PARK" your needle when you are done stitching or changing the thread</u> .

- RULE #4 - You do NOT NEED A HOOP!

- RULE #5 - Have fun—you are creating a visual art, a fiber art, a wearable art.

- RULE #6 - View this safari as an opportunity to learn about South Africa.

Oh, and when it comes to specific rules on safari, keep your hands inside the jeep, no shouting when you see an elephant, don't try and feed the animals, and most important be respectful of the animals—remember you are a visitor in their home!

Whether you are an accomplished quilter, sophisticated stitcher, awesome knitter or have never held a needle before, you will be stunned by the ease and beauty of African Folklore Embroidery. The bright colors against the black fabric create a wonderful contrast and the use of chain stitch gives the embroidery a slightly three-dimensional, raised appearance.

Like most ethnic embroidery, chain stitch is the dominant stitch in African Folklore Embroidery. Chain stitch is a very rhythmical stitch, a stitch that flows beautifully and quickly, and is easy to do while doing other things such as chatting with friends, watching television, riding on a plane or train, or watching a basketball or soccer game. I usually take an embroidery design with me wherever I go; I fold it up and put it in my

The particular "Big Five" design above, completed by Pam Ross, uses more traditional wildlife colors. The entire design is completed in chain stitch, except for the French knots used for the leopard's spots and satin stitch used for the buffalo's horns. The effectiveness of French knots and satin stitch can be seen by the filling in of the buffalo's horns and the spots on the leopard. Silver metallic thread has been used for the legs of the bugs. The use of metallic thread gives the design a hint of sparkle.

purse. In fact from being a nervous flyer, I now look forward to my travel trips as this is my time to do my African Folklore Embroidery. Since you can take needles on a plane, I have found this traveling allows me guilt-free time to pursue my favorite hobby. In fact it also relaxes me considerably during takeoff, landing and any turbulent times on board. Our first stop on our journey through South Africa will be to see animals on safari. We will begin this visual safari through a multicultural needle art called African Folklore Embroidery.

Why do most people want to go to Africa? To see "The Big Five"; elephant, leopard, lion, rhino and buffalo up close. Going to any one of a number of game parks will afford one this opportunity. The Kruger Park, one of the most famous game parks in South Africa, is home to nearly 150 species of mammals and an abundance **of wildlife and birdlife**. It would not be uncommon to spot each of "The Big Five" as well as giraffes, buck, baboons, warthogs and zebra on a single game drive.

The Kruger Park is also known for its **large lion population** and communities of cheetah and spotted hyena. Remember this is not a zoo, none of the animals are in cages; you are observing these beasts in their own natural habitat. In most of the game parks you can expect to see "The Big Five". One of my favorite game parks is Pilanesberg, about two hours outside of Johannesburg. My family and I have gone both with a ranger in an open jeep and in our car; both ways we were able to see and observe a wide variety of

The "Big Five" design above makes use of several hand-dyed variegated thread colors and chain stitch to give it impact. The tree is completed in one of my favorite African variegated colors, Harvest (64). Other variegated colors used include Hellebore (62), Lavender (34), Mango (24) and Holly (56).

animals up close and very personal. At times you can expect to see giraffe walking right alongside the car, and if in

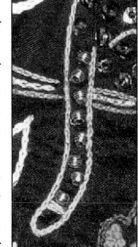

the mood, baboons and other monkeys may climb on top of your car's roof!

What you will see in this book are depictions of wildlife through African Folklore Embroidery. You will also read some of the descriptions of how the designs have been completed. While the rule is that you do not need to use authentic colors to complete a design, there is nothing to say you cannot stitch in authentic colors.

This "Big Five" design, completed by Heather Olague, makes use of chain stitch and a variety of

different beads. Heather used an old necklace that she cut up for the string beads on the elephant's body, strings of beads from a bracelet for the body of the rhino, and individual beads for the leopard's spots.

Each of the animals has been chain-stitched in a different color, making each a feature within the design. By doing the mane of the lion in blue, an extreme contrast to the purple outline, it makes the mane into a unique part of the design. The string of beads on the rhino's body draws one's eye there.

Buffalos

The buffalo, which is included in our "Big Five" design, is a very adaptable animal. They occupy open grasslands, wooded savanna and thickets. Buffalo associate in herds of up to 1,000 or more individuals. Despite being very aggressive and extremely dangerous animals (more hunters are killed by buffalos than any other animal), buffalos are very peaceful amongst themselves. The dominant bull normally is the oldest bull in the herd. Both males and females have horns, but those of males are heavier. Males can weigh up to 1,600lbs and have a life span of approximately twenty years. Buffalo are herbivores. Female buffalo are ready to mate at the age of five. The gestation period for buffalos is eleven months, after which a single calf is born.

When on safari it can be easy to mistake wildebeest for buffalo. To help you spot the difference here is some information that may be useful. A buffalo's back is straight while a wildebeest has a more sloped back. Buffalo tend to graze in wooded areas while wildebeest graze in open grassy areas. While both animals are herbivores, a buffalo more resembles a cow and a wildebeest is more similar in appearance to a gazelle. Predators of the buffalo include lion and man, while predators of the wildebeest are lions, jackals and leopards.

Leopards

Leopards can be found in areas where there are open plains and savanna, as well as in hills and rocky outcrops. Leopards normally hunt at night and dusk. They stay in secluded spots during the day or lie in high branches of trees. Leopards are solitary animals and male and female leopards only associate for mating purposes.

Leopards are masters of camouflage and will move silently through vegetation to attack their prey at very close quarters. Leopards usually kill their victim with a bite to the back of the neck, and then drag them up a tree, where they can feed at leisure, away from scavengers.

Leopards, known as the hunters of the cat family, are regarded as territorial animals and will live to about fifteen years of age. They can weigh about 150lbs. Their prey includes impala, bushbuck, warthog and also the young of wildebeest, kudu and waterbuck. Rodents, ground birds, monkeys, baboons, frogs and fish also make up part of their diet. The female gives birth to one to three cubs after a gestation period of about 105 days. The cubs are kept in secluded spots when the female leopards go hunting.

What you will observe in all the African Folklore Embroidery designs is the element of nature, the trees, grass and vegetation. These elements are fundamental to the survival and ongoing existence of all wild animals.

Lions

We are all in awe of the power and strength of lions, but let's be honest, how close do you really want to get to a real live one?

The all-powerful lion is king of the jungle and the most powerful of the African predators. With just a swipe of one of their paws, lions can break a wildebeest's neck, and they can carry twice their weight in their powerful jaws. Lions live in groups called prides. Lions are more abundant in open plains where there is permanent water and plenty of grazing, and consequently, plenty of game.

Lions, like any other cat, can see at night like humans can see during the daytime. Lions are the most social members of the cat family. They live in prides consisting of one or two males, up to seven females and fourteen to fifteen cubs of different ages. Around the age of three, young lions are evicted from their pride; these evicted lions normally stay together, always on the move, becoming nomads, until they take over some other pride, whose male has become too weak or old.

Female lions usually do all the hunting, at night, late afternoon or early morning, killing zebra, wildebeest, kudu, giraffes or even buffalo. At a kill, the adults will eat first, with the male sometimes claiming it for himself. and, if anything is left, the cubs will then take their turn. Adult males can weigh up to 500lbs. Their life span is about fifteen years.

Female lions can give birth to two to six cubs at a time, after a gestation period lasting around 110 days. The lioness normally leaves her pride and goes to a sheltered spot to give birth to her litter. She will leave her cubs to hunt and bring food to them. The mother lion will transport her cubs in her mouth and move them from one safe hideout to another.

These two lion designs have each been made into functional art, the first a quilt and the second a purse. The second one, completed by Bonnie Vorspan, allows for each leaf to be embroidered in a different solid color and the outline of the body to be completed in chain stitch using variegated shades of brown.

The lion design above on the right (purse) illustrates the use of a double outline layer. With a dark solid pink used for the outer chain-stitch border and a light pink used for a secondary border; this gives the outlines extra emphasis when there is a double outline.

If you look at this lion, you will see that the leaves have each been completed in a satin stitch in a diagonal slanted manner. Variegated color Grape(39) has been used to complete the leaves and variegated color Mango (24) has been used for chain stitch for the outline and body of the lion.

I had such fun stitching this completed lion onto the back of a black shirt; I used vibrant trim to surround the edge of the design and a selection of colors to embroider the actual design. Have you ever seen a pink sun?

13

Elephants

One of my favorite animals to observe while on safari is the elephants. I love watching the baby elephant walk in between his mom and dad and seeing how protective the moms are toward their babies. The elephant is the largest and heaviest land animal.

These beasts can weigh up to 13,000lbs and grow eleven feet in height. Elephants eat grass, leaves and fruit. They have powerful trunks that can smash down trees, branches and other vegetation such as grass, roots, reeds, fruit, bark and flowers in their path. Since elephants do not have sweat glands, water plays an important role in

their lives in helping them cool down; hence they need sources of permanent water and abundant vegetation. Elephants have a total of twenty-four teeth.

Erin Mandel used a solid pink chain stitch for the outline and light pink for the paws of the elephant above, chain-stitching the leaves in green.

Elephants are highly social animals. They live in herds, made up of the matriarch (the oldest animal in the group), her female calves and the youngsters. The herd can comprise between six and thirty animals, after which they split to form new herds, always maintaining contact with each other at watering holes and feeding spots.

At fourteen years of age, males leave the herd and associate with other bulls of the same age or older. Male elephants are much larger than female elephants with longer, heavier tusks. Elephants live for fifty to sixty years of age.

Female elephants are mature enough to mate from twelve years of age. Pregnancy/gestation is twenty-two months and a calf can weigh up to 260lbs. The calf will nurse for approximately three years.

The four completed elephant designs on this page have all been completed in their own unique style, the top two by adults and the bottom two by children. In all cases it was their first time ever holding a needle; neither the moms nor the kids had ever stitched before and they were all very surprised by their creations.

The purple elephant above, completed by Heather Olague, makes used of brown string beads cut up from a necklace that have been stitched onto the body of the elephant, and a string of black beads stitched onto the tail, giving it a

swishing effect. The rest of the design has been completed in bright solid colors in chain stitch. Each of the leaves has been tightly chain-stitched using a different solid color.

The two designs on the left were completed by children between the ages of seven and eleven. Once they got into the rhythm of the chain stitch they felt conformable completing the design and even adding beads.

Rhinos

The rhino is a member of The Big Five for which South Africa is famous. The rhino can weigh up to 5,000lbs, has horns on its face, and runs very fast. While you may never actually see a pink, blue or orange rhino, the opportunities to beautify an African Folklore Embroidery rhino are endless.

The two types of rhino are The Black Rhino and The White Rhino. The Black Rhino's head is much smaller than the white rhino. The black rhino is not a social animal, rather solitary in nature and can be aggressive. Black Rhinos prefer densely wooded areas, with lots of shrubs and plenty of water, whilst White Rhinos prefer more grassland.

A pink rhino with yellow claws and a blue rhino with blue claws is something you will not see on safari.

Rhinos are short sighted, but have a strong sense of smell and hearing. Adult males can weight up to 2,500lbs. Rhinos can live up to forty years of age. Rhinos generally eat leaves, fruit, flowers and herbs.

Pregnancy/gestation period for a female rhino lasts fifteen months and a newborn calf can weigh approximately 70lbs. All animals have a different way of treating their young; in the case of the White Rhino the calf always walks in front of the mother.

The four rhinos shown here have all been completed in their own way and look different, however chain stitch is the common denominator throughout.

I had such fun stitching the fourth design onto the back of a denim jacket. On the fourth rhino orange trim has been tacked on in a wavy vertical manner, to the body of the rhino allowing for the inclusion of other fibers into this art form, and giving the rhino a raised, three-dimensional appearance.

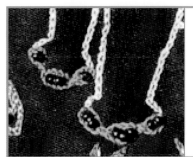

Stitching beads onto the toenails of the rhino can make the feet into beautiful features.

Hippos

The trick when you are on safari is to try and spot a hippo; hippos are not easy to spot as they are half submerged in water and because they stand so still they look like rocks. Humans are not the only ones who can be tricked into thinking these hippos are rocks; animals also are fooled to their detriment. The hippo can weigh up to 8,000lbs and swims in rivers and lakes.

The hippopotamus, or hippos as we affectionately refer to them, is the third-largest living land mammal, after elephants and white rhinos. The hippo's huge, grayish-brown body is almost hairless and is supported by short legs with four toes at the end of each foot. The hippo depends on water and mud to keep it cool. The hippo can extend up to thirteen feet in length and five feet in height. It eats grass and enjoys wading through swamps and rivers. Hippos require water deep enough to cover them, within commuting distance of a pasture. They must submerge because their thin, naked skin is vulnerable to overheating and dehydration. Female hippos can mate at the age of nine years old and are pregnant for a period of eight months.

These two hippo designs were completed by children between the ages of seven and nine, using bright solid threads and chain stitch. In both cases it was their first time attempting embroidery or stitching.

Giraffes

The tallest animal you will see roaming freely, elegantly and majestically is the giraffe. The giraffe is so graceful, growing up to nineteen feet and weighing over 4,000lbs. The giraffe's tongue can measure eighteen inches in length. With their long necks, giraffes are usually the first to spot danger and fire. The other animals keep a close eye on the giraffes to see where they are headed.

The giraffe's height allows it to keep in contact with other giraffes over large distances, as well as spot predators from afar. It is not uncommon to see other animals following a giraffe using it as an early predator warning system. The neck is so long the giraffe must spread its front legs apart so its head can reach the ground to drink. It has unusually elastic blood vessels with a series of valves that help offset the sudden buildup of blood (and to prevent fainting), when the head is raised, lowered or swung quickly.

The giraffe's high shoulders and sloping back give the impression that its front legs are much longer than the hind legs, but they are in fact only slightly longer. Giraffes are herbivores. When protected, giraffes can flourish in areas where food is abundant year round. Although they drink water when it's available, they can survive where it is scarce. Giraffes occasionally eat grass and fruits of various trees and shrubs, but their principal food source are acacia trees. The giraffe's gestation period is fifteen months and it can live to about twenty-eight years of age.

Getting Started—GIRAFFES

This section gives you step-by-step instructions for African Folklore Embroidery using the giraffe design to illustrate stitches, embellishment techniques and beading. So far our journey has exposed you to many of the animals you can expect to see on safari. After a busy day in the bushveld it's time to take out our African Folklore Embroidery designs, soak up the inspiration from the safari, and start working on our own African Folklore Embroidery designs.

Let's get started! Welcome to the colorful and creative world of African Folklore Embroidery. I am excited to have you along on this visual safari, but before we begin any design, let's once again go over the basic rules of African Folklore Embroidery:

- *Whatever color you choose to stitch is the right color—there is no wrong color; if you wish to stitch your giraffes pink or your sun blue—go for it!*

- *Your stitches do not need to be perfect—there are no needle art police who are going to come and inspect your work!*

- *The needles are only to be used for stitching, no poking anyone or sewing yourself! (obvious, but worth mentioning)*

- *You do NOT NEED A HOOP!*

- *Have fun—you are creating a visual art, a fiber art, a wearable art.*

You will see an example of what the design will look like on completion. I will take you step-by-step through this project, which is the same design I worked on for Uncommon Threads on HGTV's DIY channel (Duct-254). Most important to remember is that when it comes to African Folklore Embroidery there is no right or wrong. In this book I show you a variety of techniques and stitches to complete an African Folklore Embroidery design, but remember everybody's completed design is different. No two ever look the same; while the purpose of this book is to show you the possibilities with African Folklore Embroidery, there is nothing to say you cannot just complete the entire design in chain stitch, using none of the other techniques. However, the techniques I demonstrate in this book do show you how to enhance your overall design. Please remember that the completed giraffe design I demonstrate is just one interpretation.

The Kit Designs

The kits designed by South African artists are inspired by life in South Africa, wildlife, tribal, villages, flowers and vegetation. The fabric of the kits is known by several names—"Drill," "Twill" or "Tabeling"—but it is essentially a cotton derivative. The fabric is cut and over-locked in South Africa to prevent fraying. The reason you do not need a hoop is that the fabric is wonderfully sturdy and taut.

Since kits include the design, a needle and bright African threads, all you need is a scissors. Should you desire, you can incorporate African hand-dyed and variegated threads into your design. These multicolored threads change color every two inches and really enhance and give accent to a design. A full-color chart of the over 200 African variegated thread colors can be viewed on our website at www.aflembroidery.com. These threads, manufactured in South Africa by House of Embroidery, are beautiful and easy to use. I refer to them as eye candy. The thread dyers use the changing and varied colors in nature as their inspiration. While I suggest predominantly using threads of a pearl 8 weight, there is no reason that other thread weights and fibers cannot be incorporated into the design for accent and effect.

In fact the mixing of different types of fibers into the design makes African Folklore Embroidery into a fiber art as well as a needle art. I encourage you to view these projects as a way to incorporate other threads and fibers that you may have around your home. You can also add in beads and sequins into your design and I will show you this technique. While any beads can be used, I suggest beads with a good-sized eye, so that the needle fits through the eye of the bead.

Kit design

All of our kits include instructions, design printed on black fabric, needle and braid of brightly colored, variegated thread from South Africa.

Sun stitched in chain stitch in the giraffe design

Completed Giraffe - Design #AN-11

Bright-colored beads are great to use and form a wonderful color contrast against the black fabric. If you decide to use small seed beads you may want to use a thinner, smaller needle so that the threaded needle will fit through the eye of the bead. In the case of beads with a tiny eye, you can use beading thread to stitch on the bead. (You may want to use a tapestry needle threader to help with threading your needle). In the kit you will see either a tapestry, chenille or embroidery needle. Any of these needles can be used and it is really about the needle that you feel most comfortable working with.

Getting Started

To get started, open the plastic packaging with your kit enclosed. You will see your needle attached to your braided threads. These cotton threads are from South Africa and are a combination of pearl 5 and pearl 8 weights. You do not need to unbraid the threads. Look at your design and decide where you would like to begin and what color inspires you. I suggest starting with the outline of one of the features of the design, for example the outline of the giraffe or the outline of the sun or the tree.

Once you have chosen your thread color, pull out the thread from the top of the braid; it will come out very easily, leaving the other threads in the braid intact. Thread your needle. Use one thread at a time and do not split the thread. Since the weight of most of the threads in the braid is either a 5 or an 8, you should use them as they are, not doubling or splitting. You want to single-thread your needle and tie a knot at the end of the thread, about an inch away from the end. I like to use a quilter's knot and will show you how to do it.

Quilter's Knot

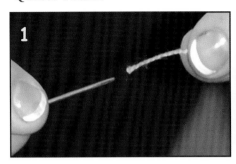  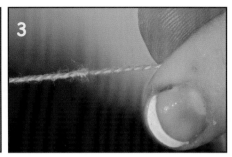

The secret with a quilter's knot is to have the point of the needle and the end piece of the thread facing each other (1). Place the tip of the thread on the middle of the needle, wrap the thread around the needle and with your other finger push the wrapped part down toward the end of the needle (2); this will create a neat knot at the end of your thread (3).

If you have a child working on one of our designs, my suggestion is to double-thread the needle and then do the quilter's knot. The double-thread for kids prevents the thread coming out of the needle and needing to be rethreaded, causing frustration. The quilter's knot is a great, easy knot to teach kids and can be used with double threading.

Once thread, remember we always start from THE BACK OF THE FABRIC.

Let's begin with outlining the sun in chain stitch. First choose a color and then thread your needle—double-thread it with a knot at the end for kids, single-thread it with a knot at the end for adults.

Chain Stitch

Chain stitch is the dominant stitch used in African Folklore Embroidery. It is an easy yet very effective and rhythmical stitch; once you are in a comfortable rhythm, it goes very quickly. I find I can do chain stitch while multitasking, such as watching TV, talking on the phone, watching my son play soccer or basketball, and still be social at the same time. Do not worry about the spacing of the stitches, as later we will use another colored thread in between the spaces.

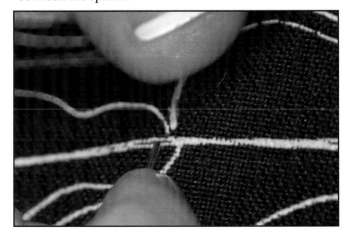 

Step-by-Step Chain Stitch

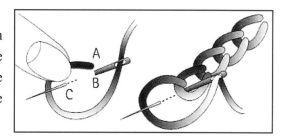

Starting with chain stitch, bring the threaded needle through the fabric at the beginning of the design, and hold it down with the left thumb. Thread the needle into the fabric from the front (where the thread last came out) and bring the point of the needle out of the fabric a short distance away.

Pull the needle through and keep working the thread under the needle point making the chain. Once you have brought your threaded needle up through the fabric from the back, you go back down into the fabric slightly behind the stitch (less than a quarter of an inch) and come back up through the fabric in front of where you first came up; thereafter set your thread up so that it is in a semi-circle in front of your needle.

This I refer to in workshops as the pond (your needle needs to be in the center of the pond because when you pull it through, it is this pond that creates the loop and chain effect). Once complete with your starting chain stitch, for your next stitch, you go back through the middle of your first stitch, come up in front (less than a quarter inch), set up your thread as a circle in front of your needle and bring your needle up through the pond. Very soon, you will be doing this motion without giving it a second thought!).

To end off your chain stitch, you want to leave about three inches of thread. What I suggest is after your last chain stitch, point your needle down into the fabric at the end of the last stitch, go through the fabric with the threaded needle, flip the kit over and using your needle, weave through the back of your last two stitches securing the stitch

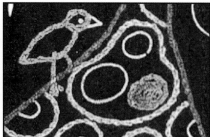

In this example I have outlined the giraffe in red and the circular spots inside in light pink to create a contrast.

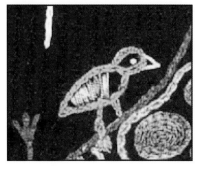

and create a knot so it does not come untied. Once you have ended off you can rethread and begin again with your chain stitch. Remember if you wish to change colors, even in the middle of doing an outline, you can! Remember that colors for stitching do not have to be authentic, so if you want to stitch the outline of your giraffe red, pink or green, go for it!

As you can see from the pictures the entire design so far has been completed using chain stitch and solid colors.

Satin Stitch

Satin stitch is a wonderful filler stitch for small areas, creating a raised, puffy appearance.

I have filled in the inside of the bird's body using a vertical satin stitch. To create a more defined satin stitch area, I suggest bordering the area with chain stitch and then using a different color to fill in with the satin stitch.

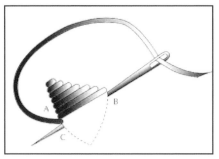

Coming from the back of the fabric, we will fill the body using straight stitches, next to each other, to create a smooth satin effect.

I have completed the hooves of the giraffe using a horizontal satin stitch. Depending on the direction of the satin stitch—horizontal, vertical or diagonal—it can take on a different effect. What can make satin stitch more effective is to outline the area in a solid chain stitch and then use a variegated thread to fill in the open space with satin stitch.

One can also do the reverse and use a solid color to fill in the small defined area in satin and then a variegated thread to outline the area in a chain stitch. Below is the outline of the bird that has been chain-stitched in solid blue, while the inside has been filled in using variegated color Peacock (38) in satin stitch.

Because the colors change every two inches, even using a small amount of thread for a limited area, one will see the multiple color changes.

A hand-dyed variegated pearl 8 thread called Freesia (48) has been used to complete the trunk and branches of the trees.

A solid color is used for the branches, which makes the variegated thread stand out even more.

21

Examples of different applications and variations of satin stitch to fill a small area can be seen below. Vertical satin stitch has been used to fill in the circles and horizontal satin stitch has been used to fill in the squares. Both sets of circles have been outlined in a solid blue stem stitch and the variegated color Freesia (48) has been used for satin stitch. Lines of satin stitch in different solid colors and variegated colors create an interesting effect.

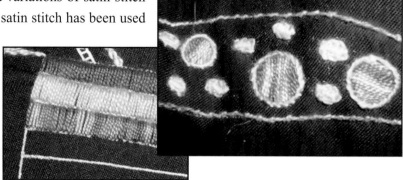

Stem/Back Stitch

Using a hand-dyed variegated thread, we are going to introduce a new stitch into our design—stem stitch. This stitch is used for stems and outlines. It can also be used as a filling stitch where rows of stem stitches worked closely together fill the design. We work from left to right taking small, even straight or slightly slanted, stitches along the design lines. Leave a space where the needle emerges and the previous stitch ends. The thread should always come out on the left side of the previous stitch.

The grass between the giraffe's legs has been completed using stem stitch in a variegated color called Forest (54). A hand-dyed variegated pearl 8 thread called Freesia (48) has been used to complete the trunk and branches of the trees. A solid color is used for the branches which makes the variegated thread stand out even more.

French Knots

The flowers on the side of the plants make a great area for French knots. French knots can be used as filler stitches for small areas, creating depth, height and dimension. For example you can fill in the ears of the giraffe or the small circles inside the giraffe's body. French knots assist in creating a three-dimensional, raised appearance. To do French knots bring the thread through the fabric at the position required.

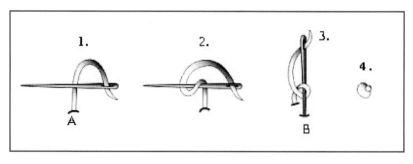

Hold the thread taut with the thumb and place the needle on top of the thread. Then wrap the thread around the needle two to four times. Still holding the thread firmly, put the needle back into the fabric, close to where the thread first emerged.

To create French knots that give the appearance of beads, one can wrap the threads five or more times to create a thicker French knot with more depth, width and height.

Embellishment Techniques

Beading

Beads and bead art is an integral part of African tribal customs. In Ndebele culture, children wear beads before they wear clothes, and girls will learn intricate beadwork from their mothers. Dolls, necklaces, key rings and other artifacts made by the tribes are intricately beaded, and other beaded items are sold to tourists and form the main source of income for many tribal women. In African culture, beading is not only used for decoration, but the actual beading can convey messages of love and courtship. Young girls will send personalized beaded messages to their "chosen" men. Different color combinations imply different types of messages and meaning. Color combinations can be used to communicate pregnancy, marriage, engagements, birth of a child, and death or grief.

Beading is a wonderful embellishment to an African Folklore Embroidery design. There can be obvious places for beads within the design, such as the eye of an animal or person, or a string of beads for a tail, or go crazy with beads and embellish and stitch beads anywhere. From the designs in this book, you can already see how beadwork has been incorporated into African Folklore Embroidery designs. There are two ways beads can be used in African Folklore Embroidery.

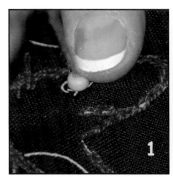 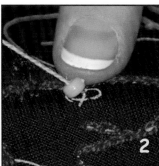 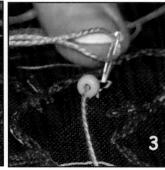

Attaching a single bead

Beads can be individually stitched onto the design. To do this, thread your needle and tie a knot at the end of the thread. If you wish you can use the same or a similar color thread as the bead, however this is not essential. Push the needle up from the fabric at the desired location for the bead and place the bead on top of the needle, then bring the needle through the eye of the bead, and secure the bead by going down into the fabric on the side of the bead. If the eye is big enough one can secure the bead on both sides of the eye of the bead. The same technique for attaching beads can be used for sequins and buttons.

 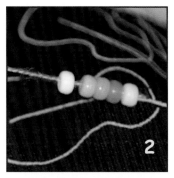

Attaching a string of beads

Thread the needle, tie a knot, push the needle through the fabric, place several beads on the needle (1), bring the needle through the eyes of all the beads, lay the beads flat and push the needle down into the fabric at the end of the last bead (4). Then secure the beads by interweaving at the back. If one wishes for the beads to be extra secure and tight, one can couch in between the beads (6).

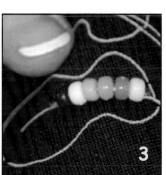  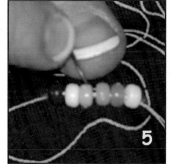 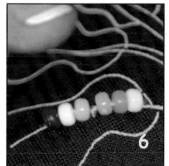

Interweaving

There are three interweaving techniques that can be incorporated into your design. We will discuss and demonstrate each of these techniques and show their application.

- Mola Barbara Interweaving Technique

- Double-Sided Interweaving Technique

- Roller Coaster

Feel free to use different fibers for interweaving, such as silk ribbon to create extra texture.

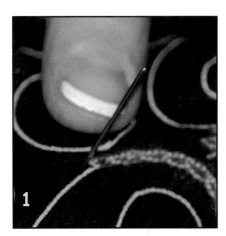 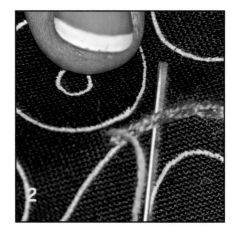 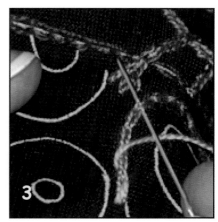

Mola Barbara Interweaving Technique (MBIT)

The Mola Barbara is an easy, quick technique to enhance your design and give it a three-dimensional, raised, rope-like appearance. The chain stitch is the foundation for any of the embellishment, wrapping and interweaving techniques. Once you have completed your chain stitch, choose another color thread and thread your needle with a knot at the end. Bring your threaded needle up at the side of the chain stitch (1) (either side is okay), then wrapping in diagonally wrap the chain stitch every stitch or every other stitch (2). You are not going into the black fabric, purely wrapping the chain stitch (3). Continue doing this until the outline is completely wrapped.

The overall effect of this technique is one that looks extremely striking and three-dimensional. When people see your work they are going to wonder how you did it and you will be amazed at how quick and easy this is!

Double-Sided Interweaving Technique

Once again using the chain stitch as your foundation, choose and thread another color thread. Coming up from the back of the fabric, using just the one side of the chain stitch (2), wrap the thread though one side of the stitch, go all the way up and then go down the other side of the stitch either in the same color or a different color thread (4).

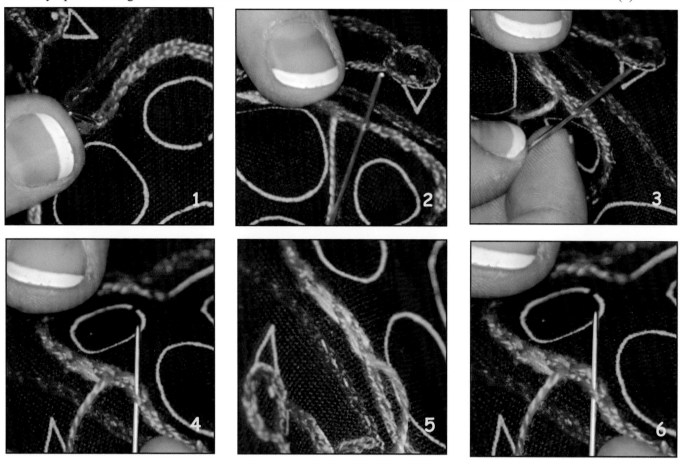

Roller Coaster

Once again using the chain stitch as a foundation, thread your needle with a different colored or variegated thread. Bring your threaded needle up in the middle of the chain stitch (7), go down in the middle of the next stitch and then bring your needle up in the middle (8). The effect of the roller coaster technique is to create a hint of another color or texture (9).

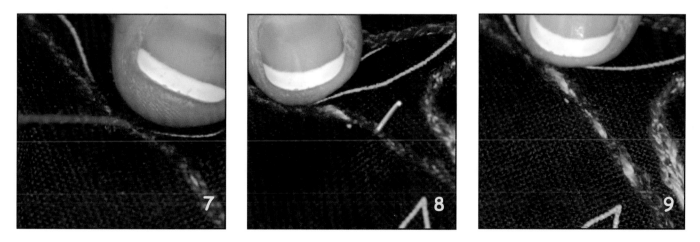

When it comes to doing your African Folklore Embroidery design, imagine yourself as an artist, and start playing with threads and colors. Here are some examples of how you can play with threads and colors just using a basic up-down running stitch, the foundation of the satin stitch.

Criss-cross stitch

Doing a cross stitch and then using a different color thread to couch where the threads touch or connect, creates an interesting and varied contrast within the design.

These pictures illustrate the criss-cross stitch using different shades of variegated green, such as Cabbage (30), Holly (56), Lemon & Lime (25), Periwinkle (7), Fern (4), Bush (8) and Foxtail (79).

On this giraffe we used only chain stitch and incorporated different shades of hand-dyed variegated purple threads. Everything is filled in using chain stitch.

Different Interpretations of the Same Giraffe

Completed in bright solid colors using chain stitch. Every part of the design, including the sun, has been filled in with the chain stitch.

This design was completed by a nine-year-old boy. It was his first attempt at stitching, he loved being able to choose his colors and mastered chain stitch very well.

Fabric-Fiber-Beading Fusion

Continuing with our safari through African Folklore Embroidery let us see how we can incorporate fibers, fabric, appliqué and beads to make our designs into fiber art. Since the designs are pre-drawn, this is the perfect project for any extra scraps and pieces of fabric, since quilters usually have huge stashes of beautiful fabric; those hard-to-throw -away pieces can be incorporated, enhancing their beauty even more.

Fabric-Fiber-Beading-Appliqué Fusion Through African Folklore Embroidery

Asking quilters whether they have a stash of fabric or any pieces of material that they love but do not want to get rid of is like asking whether a cat has a tail! Ask a knitter if they have some wool or yarn lying around and they may just laugh. African Folklore Embroidery is the perfect craft to bring in all those small pieces of fabrics, fibers, beads, buttons and other small items lying around the house that you do not want to get rid of. Even an old necklace that is no longer worn can be cut up and incorporated into your design, making your African Folklore Embroidery design a real fiber art project.

The Ndebele lady and house design (AF23) above appeared on PBS Television show, The Needle Arts Studio. I stitched on large wooden African beads to fill in the roof of the house. For the door, I stitched on a piece of fabric using a green bead as the door knob. African Fiber Art is about using everyday common objects from our environment, recycling and converting them into an art form. Variegated brown silk ribbon has been used for the outline of the house and this ribbon has been couched down using satin stitch. The windows have been filled in with the wooden African beads, displayed in a vertical manner. Above the windows, I used silk ribbon from a gift bag that I stitched onto the top of the house. The rooster has been completely filled in with colored beads, and metallic gold thread has been used to stitch the crown of the rooster. Triangular pieces of orange fabric interspersed with beads have been stitched into each of the four corners of the design. The middle-sized chicken has a sequin stitched on for its eye and the baby chicken is completed with yellow fabric. Brown bullion stitch has been used to represent the corn. I had such fun completing the dresses of the ladies, using scraps of fabric. Gold metallic thread was used for the necklace.

I call the next design "Beaded Bodacious Ostrich," because as you can see I went really crazy with beads on the ostrich design (B21). Bead lovers know that beads can really add a fun and colorful element to a design, turning needle art into bead art. Aside from stitching on beads individually within this design, I also incorporated two sets of beaded spectacle strings made by the women from Kidzpositive, South Africa. These were easy to attach using couching. These beaded spectacle strings can be found on www.aflembroidery.com.

The sun on the ostrich design has been made into a real feature, with both extensive chain stitch and strings of beads for the sun rays. Clusters of gold beads have been used to fill in the inside of the sun. The Mola Barbara Interweaving Technique has been used for the leaf on the right-hand side, using green silk ribbon to interweave the chain stitch. Each leaf has been filled in using a different colored thread. Each of the spots and circles on the body of the ostrich has been completed in their own way. Some have been outlined in a solid chain stitch and filled in with satin stitch; others have been completed with clusters of beads.

Using the fish design as an example, our safari journey will take you through how you can go about incorporating fabric into your design using only the kit you have, a pair of scissors, some pins, a marker, and some scraps of fabric. This also allows for the project to be transportable and a great take-along for vacations, road-trips and travel excursions.

Method for Including Fabric into Your African Folklore Embroidery Design

Arrange fabric pieces on the design according to your choice of colors and preference. While the design is still in the plastic packaging, using a marker outline the parts of the fish on which you wish to appliqué fabric.

Now remove the design from the packaging and using a scissors cut out the marked outline on the plastic packaging.

Take the cutout plastic pieces and place onto the fabric pieces you have selected, (make sure the selected fabric is folded so you will get two sides of the fabric), then cut out the fabric according to the shape you have outlined on the plastic packaging.

Turn the cutout piece of fabric inside out and stitch the sides together, leaving a small opening so that you can turn the fabric inside out. Once complete, place the cutout piece of fabric on the design where you would like it to be incorporated and pin it to the design. Then, thread your needle with either the same or similar color to the fabric.

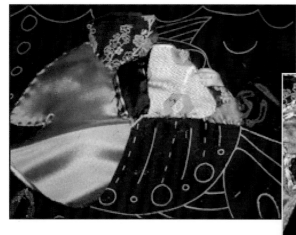

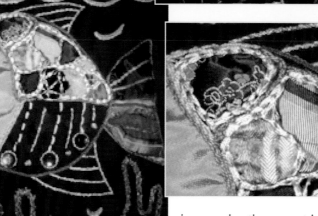

Using chain stitch or alternatively a running satin stitch, stitch the cutout piece of fabric onto the design. If you wish you can leave a small opening so that if you desire you can place batting, wool or other fibers underneath the fabric to make it stand out and give the design a three-dimensional feel.

The advantage of this type of appliqué and fabric incorporation is that the design is already drawn on the black fabric, so there is no major time spent in preparing for the appliqué process.

28

Silk Ribbon and Couching

If you would like to utilize the silk ribbon and couching technique in your design, thread your needle (you may wish to use a needle with a bigger eye for threading silk ribbon) and tie a knot at the end of the ribbon. Coming up from the behind the fabric, bring your threaded silk ribbon needle. Lay out the silk ribbon on the area over which you intend for it to be couched and secure. At the end of the area, bring your needle down into the fabric and secure. Then using regular thread, either solid or variegated, bring your needle up on the side of the ribbon, go down through the fabric on the other side of the silk ribbon, leave a space of less than a quarter inch, and repeat the technique along the silk ribbon. This couching technique can also be done in a criss-cross manner as has been demonstrated in the picture on the left.

Fibers and Needle Felting in African Folklore Embroidery

If you enjoy needle felting, you can incorporate needle felting into the design. As you can see in the fish below, various fibers and wools have been fused into the design using needle-felting techniques. The butterfly design demonstrates the use of pink yarn interwoven, using the Mola Barbara Interweaving Technique, into the middle section of the butterfly, creating a fuzzy and furry appearance.

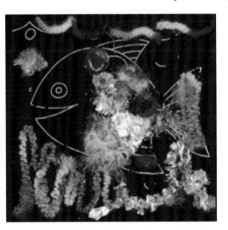
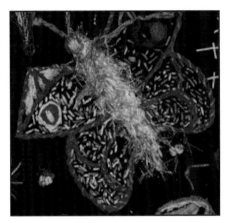

Examples of Making African Folklore Embroidery Into Fiber Art

In this design, completed by Connie Anderson, you will see that actual pine needle sticks have been used for the roof of the house. Interspersed between the pine needles is brown chain stitch. Fabric appliqué has been incorporated into both dresses and both women have strings of beads as their necklaces. Beads form an integral part of this design, featured throughout on the branches of the tree, the sun, the ladies' legs, and their dresses. Using the Mola Barbara Interweaving Technique, blue wool fiber has been interwoven into the outline of the bird. Tight brown bullion stitch has been used for the hair.

Each of the pine needles used has been carefully couched down with brown thread.

29

The following two examples are completed in very different ways. Connie Anderson completed the one on the right and I completed the one below. The roof of the house almost looks like it is fabric, but if you look closely you will see that Connie has outlined the roof in chain stitch using variegated color Maple (65) and then chain-stitched vertically and horizontally using the same color. Where the chain stitches connect she has filled those squares with satin stitch using variegated color Mango (24). The Ndebele lady's dress incorporates fabric as well as variations of satin stitch. The bottom two layers of the dress are stitched in vertical satin stitch, with each line in a different shade of pink, creating a striking contrast. Bullion stitch has been used in the hair and sprinkles of beads are interspersed with the chickens.

Doing the design on the left I wanted to highlight the beadwork done by mothers from Kidzpositive in South Africa, and also use a variety of different fiber mediums. You can see a beaded bookmark on the left of the design and three beaded key chains interspersed in the design, with one forming the door of the house. What makes this design different to other completed designs is that the entire design, including the black background, has been filled in using both chain stitch and trims.

This design makes use of chain stitch and satin stitch, solid thread, metallic and variegated threads. Thatch rope intertwined on top of the chain stitch has been used for the border of the design. Fabric has been appliquéd into the dress. The paper on the design explains the work that Kidzpositive does in creating employment for mothers with AIDS.

Stranded Floss, Silk Ribbon, Metallics and Other Interesting Fibers

What I love about doing African Folklore Embroidery is that one never gets bored. The same design can be completed so differently by each person. Using threads that you may have around the house, such as stranded floss can add a new depth and dimension to one's design. The choice of threads that one incorporates will define the overall texture of the embroidery. It is texture that differentiates embroidery from other art forms, and a design can include more than one texture—a flat texture and a raised texture (for example by using a thicker thread weight or bullion or French knots).

We can add sparkle to our design by using metallic threads, and we can give our design a silk matted appearance by using either fine or raw silk thread. Using variegated threads allows us to accent our design by incorporating many shades of the same solid color. Rayon threads can also give the design a certain luster and shine. Rayon, silk and metallic can be slippery to work with, so it helps to tie a knot at the eye of the needle. Many metallic threads come in stranded form; one can use the thread as is, or split into one or a few pieces, depending on how fine or delicate a metallic appearance one wants to give the design.

Blending Fibers

In creating a unique feature within a design one can combine fibers of different types and use them in the same needle. For example doing chain stitch with a hand-dyed variegated pearl 8 thread and a string of metallic simultaneously creates an interesting effect. The rule of thumb is to cut both threads the same length. Using a thicker metallic can give the appearance of a rope or cord on the design.

African Threads

All hand-dyed and variegated threads used in African Folklore Embroidery come from South Africa. These hand-dyed threads are cotton and initially gray. They are then washed, boiled and rewashed. Thereafter with a teaspoon a different color is poured on the thread

every two inches. The threads are then washed and fan dried to ensure they are light, color and wash fast. The purchase of these threads assists in creating valuable employment opportunities for women in South Africa.

Many of the women involved in the thread-dyeing and packaging process have been able to move from informal shack housing to formal housing with running water and electricity. There are over 200 variegated colors and each color is taken through all the thread fibers.

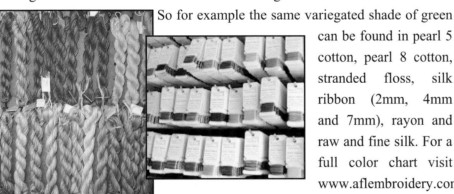

So for example the same variegated shade of green can be found in pearl 5 cotton, pearl 8 cotton, stranded floss, silk ribbon (2mm, 4mm and 7mm), rayon and raw and fine silk. For a full color chart visit www.aflembroidery.com.

African Tribal Traditions and Customs

Our safari through African Folklore Embroidery now continues, taking us to meet the people who make up the "rainbow nation." With South Africa's eleven official languages and population of approximately forty-eight

million, it is a country rich and diverse in culture and tradition. Each tribe in South Africa has its own language, customs and traditions. Many of the African Folklore Embroidery designs are inspired by the customs and traditions of the Ndebele tribe. Before I go any further I would like to teach you how to say the word Ndebele; it sounds like "in the belly" but pronounced with an N—Ndebele, "In-da belly." Although they are one of the smallest tribes in South Africa, their fame is routed in their beautiful beadwork and colorful handcrafted and beaded dolls. The Ndebele

women are known throughout the world for their bold colors and mural art, such as the painting of the outside of their houses in bright colors.

The Ndebele people were originally an offshoot of the Nguni people of KwaZulu-Natal. Around the 1600s the Ndebele tribe lived in Pretoria (north of Johannesburg). After their king—King Musi—died, a fierce fight broke out between his two sons, Manala and Ndzundza. This led to bloodshed. After many years of strife, they decided to live apart, the Manala in the Pretoria area and the Ndzundza further east. In the 1820s Mzilikazi, a Zulu general, fleeing from Shaka, overpowered the Manala and decided to settle down with them. After some time, Mzilikazi became afraid that Shaka would send an army after him. He moved to and settled in Zimbabwe. That is the origin of the Ndebele of Zimbabwe. In 1984 when the KwaNdebele Homeland was established, many Ndebele made it their home.

In lectures, workshops and classes adults and children learn about the history and culture of the Ndebele tribe in South Africa through African Folklore Embroidery.

While African Folklore Embroidery is a form of needlework, it is also a visual and cultural art that develops positive self-esteem and creativity in children, allowing them to be exposed to other cultures. Beadwork is one of the oldest and most basic decorative arts practiced by the Ndebele people.

Art forms such as painting, doll making and bead crafts are passed down from mother to daughter. There are several types of Ndebele beaded dolls and each one has a different symbolic meaning.

I would like to share with you some of the customs and traditions of the Ndebele tribe. Traditionally the Ndebele social structure is patriarchal with descent traced through senior men and access to the spirit worlds is through male ancestors. However it is the women who are responsible for the art and beadwork, which is symbolic of the Ndebele tribe. Through beadwork and wall paintings, women have found a creative outlet for their views, aspirations and identity.

Beadwork, Clothing and Life Stages

Beads are an important part of Ndebele culture. Beads are used to decorate or even form clothing. Ndebele children wear beads before they wear clothes. Children will wear their first beads shortly after their birth as a symbol of good luck; a simple string of white beads is worn around their waist. As they get older, beaded anklets, wristlets and necklets are worn with a fringed loin flap (*igapi*).

Very young children wear an *igabe*, which is a fringed apron with a beaded waistband featuring a design of triangles. Once girls reach puberty they will wear an *isiphephetu*, a young woman's apron.

A bride wears an *itshogolo*, a goatskin-front apron with the lower edge cut into approximately five hand-length flaps. The five flaps are symbolic of the five heads of cattle that form part of her *lobola* or dowry. The apron is worn un-beaded for her wedding, but as soon as she is married this becomes beaded in tones of blues, greens and purples. This apron is worn at important ceremonies like the initiation of her sons.

Another type of apron worn by married women is called the *amaphotto*. It has a central beaded fringe with two squared-off flaps on either side. An important item worn by brides is the *naga*, which is a splendid paneled skin cloak. This may be heavily decorated with white beads. Blankets with particular patterns are also used as cloaks and their large size provides the basis for some of the most intricate demonstrations of Ndebele bead art.

Beadwork ornaments are worn by all on the head, neck, waist, arms and legs, and may vary according to the age and status of the wearer. The *isigolwana* is a beaded ring made on the body of the wearer and cannot be removed easily.

Ndebele Customs

The Ndebele tribe has survived because of their adherence to tribal customs and lore, such as men's initiation rites, girl's puberty seclusion, first fruits ceremonies, marriage ceremonies and *lobola* feasts.

Initiation ceremonies in Ndebele culture are a celebration of manhood. Men between the ages of eighteen and twenty-two are sent away to attend circumcision schools also known as *wela*. These schools are temporary grass shelters on hilltops. They are attended by an average of ten initiates and two elders appointed by the chief discipline the initiates and teach them tribal lore. The young men learn their responsibilities toward their families and their tribe, and the means of dealing with forces that threaten tribal existence.

They also receive instruction in the traditional dress worn by women. During the three-month seclusion the young men are painted with white clay—for purity, but also to make them unrecognizable. They are smeared with animal fat and wear hide skirts, softened and stitched by their families to protect them from subzero winter cold. Painful whip fights harden them and songs of praise give them courage. These events create a strong bond among the men.

Before the young men leave for *wela*, the young women re-plaster the outside walls of their home and reconstruct the entrance ways. They then paint and repaint each year their impressions of everyday life interspersed with geometrical designs on the wall surfaces. While the young men are away at *wela* the young women throw their homes open to visitors and relatives who travel from faraway places. A white flag hoisted on a pole outside the front entrance signifies that the mother has a son at *wela*.

The women during *wela*

During *wela* the women spend most of their time adorning themselves and attending ceremonies. For such festivities an entire cow or sheep will be slaughtered and stewed in a huge three-legged cauldron for a feast that includes maize meal (pap), sour milk and sorghum beer. The women also perform ritual dancing and wave beaded sticks.

Girls and puberty

When girls reach puberty they too are secluded for three months. During this time in the privacy of their own home they perfect the art of beadwork and painting.

I have included some photographs from a recent trip to South Africa. A traditional Ndebele house where the outside walls have been painted by the women of the tribe in bright colors.

For special ceremonies, an Ndebele woman will sit outside her self-painted house, dressed in appropriate beaded status—a *linga kobe* on her head, an *isigolwana* around her neck, an *itshogolo* apron and a beaded blanket, and carry a beaded dancing stick.

I had such fun working on these four different Ndebele village designs. I found the whole process extremely relaxing and creative. I mainly used chain stitch, solid and variegated colors, such as Freesia (48) to complete it. When I had completed all four squares, I had it pieced and quilted into a wall hanging which hangs in my living room. The designs in this picture are AF10, AF12, AF18 and AF19.

The design below, *Two Sisters* (AF26), was completed by Lia Smith. In authentic Ndebele style, beads have been stitched on the legs and dress of the two Ndebele ladies.

Many Ndebele families will have chickens running around outside their house and corn in the garden. Elements of village life are depicted in the designs. Corn is an integral part of their daily food source and is used for "pap," a type of porridge, as well as for brewing beer. Lia used elongated beads stitched in a vertical manner to illustrate the beads adorned on the legs and the authentic importance of beads in Ndebele culture.

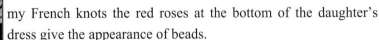

I truly enjoyed completing the design on the left (AF21). I wanted to really show the simplicity and the effect of only using solid bright colors, with chain stitch and just a few beads. I used gold and silver stranded metallic for the necklaces on both the mother and daughter. By wrapping eight times with my French knots the red roses at the bottom of the daughter's dress give the appearance of beads.

This design was completed by Minette Selling using chain stitch and beads in the hair. Beads have been stitched on individually and for the child a string of beads has been included. The leaves on the tree have been outlined and some completed using the hand-dyed African variegated threads. The tightness of the chain stitch and the sense of filling in almost everything create a beautiful overall design. The necklace and the lady's dress have been stitched using satin stitch in a vertical movement. Certain parts of the design have been filled in with row upon row of chain stitch, such as the roof of the house, the chickens and the dress. A string of beads has been used for the middle of the body of the lower butterfly. Hints of green metallic thread have been incorporated into the body of the bird.

AF22, completed by Taffy Stern, uses strings of multicolored beads for the rooftop and beads for the fish's tail, leaf stems and part of the dress. The grass has been tightly filled in with chain stitch. This is a good example of beadwork and embroidery fused and incorporated together. The village designs have been completed in chain stitch using a wide selection of variegated colors for enhancement and accent. In the second example of AF22 the use of different colored French knots in the hair gives the appearance of beads.

Even though this design (AF23) is a less detailed design, it is one of my favorite and each part of the design has been made into a feature. The sun has been chain-stitched using variegated threads which allow for the different shades of light to be reflected. The necklace on the Ndebele lady has been completed in chain stitch using three different metallic thread colors. Sequins with beads placed on top have been used for the eyes as well as the top part of the dress. The four lines below the sequins have been stitched in blue metallic and cotton thread; using spaces in between the satin stitch, metallic thread has been satin-stitched in between.

Looking at the pointed half triangles below, you will see that each side has been stitched in purple satin stitch and at the point a small yellow French knot has been stitched. The next two lines make use of variegated chain stitch and in between these two lines the criss-cross stitch is used in blue as a filler. The rooster has been outlined and then filled in using chain stitch and my favorite variegated color, Freesia (48). The rooster's beak has been filled in with satin stitch and the crown filled in with orange satin stitch. Looking at the hair of this Ndebele lady, you can see single attached beads outlined with black bullion stitch. Interwoven into the bullion stitch is a single strand of gold metallic thread.

AF23, completed by Taffy Stern, uses clusters of beads in vertical lines to fill the windows and clusters of beads in horizontal strings for the bottom of the dress. The lady's necklace has been outlined in solid blue chain stitch and then filled in with light blue tight satin stitch. If you look carefully at the small

chickens you can see they have been filled in with small tight French knots, giving them a three-dimensional appearance.

Jeanette Wahl used variegated color Freesia (48) to complete the branches of the guitar tree in the picture to the left. Individual beads and strings of beads have been stitched into the hair, making the hair a central feature of the design. The roof of the house is also a feature within the design due to the rows of chain stitch in different colors which create an interesting contrast and effect.

I love the way Analee has filled in every part of the design on the left, using chain stitch, from the house to the dresses to the trees. Depending on whether one just does the outlines of the design in chain stitch, or whether one fills in everywhere in the design in chain stitch, the completed design takes on a different dimension.

One of my favorite designs is the three ladies with the elephant and the house with beads on the dress, in the hair, and in the necklace. Satin stitch in variegated color Freesia (48) has been used to fill the inside of the dress. Bullion stitch interwoven with silver metallic thread has been used for the hair of the youngest girl.

The center of the butterfly has been completed using a string of beads. The legs of the youngest girl have been completed using silver metallic thread and horizontal chain stitch. If you look carefully at the baby chicken you can see it has been filled in completely with small French knots, giving it a three-dimensional appearance. Red metallic thread has been used for the duck's body.

The design on the left was created by Malka Dubowsky. Malka used beads to create a three-dimensional work of art, creating a colorful and striking effect.

This design was created by Taffy Stern.

Taffy used a wide selection of individual beads, in the hair and on the dresses. She used strings of blue beads for the roof of the house and used her own initiative to stitch in curtains into the windows of the house.

These two designs were completed by Shirley Hanchett. Shirley went above and beyond the scope of the design, even stitching in her own flowers and flowerpots around the windows of the house.

African Arts & Crafts

No visit to South Africa would be complete without getting to know, view and experience the amazing arts and crafts made by the people of South Africa. Each tribe has their own specialty art form that has been cultivated and passed down through the generations. The common denominator amongst these art forms is that they are made by hand with natural resources found in the environment. Today in rural areas of South Africa, people create art out of indigenous materials, such as clay, wood and

grass. From these they make and decorate items for household purposes such as serving spoons, silverware and bowls. Beading of these items is very common and is a craft practiced by many in Southern Africa.

Some rural communities even create art out of recycled items such as soda cans. Traditionally the men do most of the wood carving and the women the beading. Women make most of the items that are sold commercially, and they do this while raising their children at home in the rural communities while their husbands work in the cities. Many of these women are now being encouraged by development agencies to produce work for outside markets to be sold in the rest of the world—an example of this are the Ndebele hand-beaded dolls. The custom of carving artifacts associated with rituals is common throughout Africa. Drums and other musical instruments are commonly made by men, however in ceremonies such as weddings they are played by the women.

Basket Weaving, Pot Making—The Zulu People

Similar to quilting, basket weaving reflects the personal feelings and interpretations of the weaver. Basketry is an art form practiced by the largest tribe in South Africa, the Zulu people. This craft dates backs 200 years when tribe members began turning dried grass into functional objects, such as storage containers, cups and bowls for the household. Baskets and pots are an important part of African tribal life. The brewing of beer in these baskets, along with the sharing of beer at tribal celebrations, is an integral part of tribal life. Basket weaving, techniques and patterns are an art form passed down from one generation to the next. While the weaving methods for Zulu baskets are the same, no two baskets are alike. Grass baskets can take up to six months to complete. Leaves and grass must first be gathered, cut and dried before weaving can commence.

Since only natural dyes made from grass, berries, roots, mud and ashes are used, it can be challenging to incorporate colors such as brown, yellow and black into the basket. To produce colors such as brown and black, the weaver crushes the root of the *Isizimane* tree and boils it for several days, till the color reaches the needed intensity. The most important part of the basket is its base. Grasses and leaves cut in strips are stitched tightly around a core of coarser grass that spirals from the base to the lid. The designs and colors represent the African bush and important aspects of Zulu life, such as a diamond pattern interwoven which represents femininity, or triangles which represent the groom and a marriage. Weavers' grass baskets will differ considerably in size and design. Traditionally it was men who did the basket weaving, but as men moved to commercial jobs in the city, this became the work of the women.

In making pots, Zulu people do not use a potter's wheel to create the roundness. They grind clay very finely, using a stone while kneading it with water to form a paste and roll it into long strips. These strips are then placed and molded on top of each other to form the desired shape. The edges of the pots are smoothed with a blunt object, and then the pot is baked in a fire till it is hardened and turns a reddish-brown color. Rural women in South Africa usually carry pots on their heads. Many women learn the art of carrying pots on their head at an early age from their mothers and other female relatives. Other types of pots or baskets are used as drinking bowls and for storage, and can be designed and decorated in different styles from one community to another.

The Zulu people reside predominantly in KwaZulu-Natal. They identify with their military history; fearless fighting was exhibited by their warrior king, King Shaka, who instilled in them courage and pride. Zulus love music and music is an important part of all their ceremonies, especially string instruments, drums and wind instruments. Zulus educate the younger generation about their rich history through music and dance. Drums are made using hollowed logs, covered in tightly stretched cowhide. Zulus are very strong on displaying respect for one's elders and this is the cornerstone of their values. The Zulu tribe wears fur and stitching to adorn their bodies for ritual ceremonies, and they are well known for making spears and shields. They handcraft a long throwing spear with a small blade for hunting and men carry fighting sticks.

Cultural Traditions amongst the Zulu Tribe

Before entering a Zulu village it is customary to shout out the greeting *uku-Khuleka*. This identifies the guest and indicates that they come in friendship. In Zulu culture, wealth is measured in cattle. Cattle are also used for *Ilobola*, the dowry or bride price. The dowry is usually more than eleven heads of cattle. Zulu custom when setting out to travel on a long journey is to spit on a stone and then to throw it away. This is to ward off any evil spirits that may be tempted to come on the journey and to evoke good luck and good fortune on the journey.

In a traditional Zulu village, the house or beehive-shaped hut of the grandmother is known as the *Indlu-Nkulu*; this hut is the most important in the homestead and is decorated with the skulls of animals. The Zulus emphasize tremendous respect to the grandmothers in their tribes and families. The beehive-shaped huts are handcrafted, and usually built in a circle, surrounding their cattle (their main asset).

Clay Figurines

Many in the Venda Tribe are well known for their clay figurines and also for their wood carvings.

Doll Making

Doll making is one of the most ancient arts practiced by African communities. The Ndebele tribe are the most well known for this art form. The Zulu women also produce beautiful dolls. Most of the fertility dolls are covered in beads, but the core remains invisible. The core may be made out of cobs from corn-on-the-cob, clay or even recycled cans and jars. The Tsonga dolls are dressed in layered cloth skirts similar to those worn by the Tsonga women. All dolls generally represent married women wearing traditional forms of dress.

Doll Making and the Ndebele Tribe

The Ndebele, one of the smallest tribes in South Africa, are easily the most colorful and distinctive. Artistic beadwork is one of the oldest and most elemental of the decorative arts, which among the Ndebele tell stories of life from infancy to death. Beadwork worn during different life stages indicates the individual's status within the community. Hand-beaded dolls made by Ndebele women symbolize the different life stages.

Ndebele Initiation Doll

This doll is made in the traditional dress of a married woman. The style of the apron signifies that she has borne a child within wedlock and symbolizes her status as a parent.

Ndebele Maiden Doll

The style of the apron on this doll signifies that the girl has undergone her puberty rites and is now of marriageable age. A beaded black hoop around the waist indicates that she is engaged to be married.

Ndebele Sangoma Doll

Among the Nguni people the Sangoma is an important specialist, a diviner who claims contact with ancestral spirits. It is believed that she receives the will of the spirits. The Sangoma is referred to as the protector of society and her opinion and judgment are highly valued.

Ndebele Fertility Doll

Fertility is of major importance to the Ndebele people. A fertility doll is made (in secret) for the bride by the maternal grandmother and is ritually presented to her when she enters her new hut after the wedding ceremony. According to custom, after the birth of the third child, the fertility doll must be given away or destroyed because it is considered unlucky to keep it any longer.

Ndebele *Linga Kobe* Doll

Every four years, hundreds of Ndebele boys spend two winter months in a secret place in the mountains undergoing the *wela*, their initiation from boyhood to manhood. During this time the mothers of the initiates wear *linga kobe*, strips of beadwork that stretch from their headdresses to the ground, to show that their sons are away in the mountains. *Linga koba* translated means 'long tears'—tears of sadness at losing a boy and tears of joy at gaining a man.

Ndebele Ceremonial Doll

During courtship, a suitor would place a doll outside a young woman's hut indicating his intention to propose marriage to her.

Ndebele Bride Doll

This doll is in the traditional dress of an Ndebele bride. The panels of her apron are symbolic of the deposit of five heads of cattle toward the *lobola* (bride price). She wears a beaded train (*inyoga*), which hangs from her shoulders. Her face is covered by a beaded veil called a *siyaya*.

Zulu Basket Designs

These Zulu basket designs completed by Lynette Hasson are true works of art. Lynette, a South African native living in Los Angeles, has collected Zulu baskets for many years and was inspired by the colors and patterns within the designs when she did the embroidery. These designs use muted hand-dyed and variegated threads from Africa. The multi-coloration of the threads are reflective of the subtle changes in nature.

Lynette used the following hand-dyed African variegated thread colors to complete her design: Brass (47), Mango (24), Fern (4), Coppertone (37), Cloves (55), The Sea (36) and Harvest (64). Satin stitching has been carefully completed in a vertical manner in three distinct places within basket design a. Lynette used brassy gold beads and French knots for the upper half of the basket. The combination of the French knots and the beads make the beads highly effective. The different angles at which the chain stitch has been completed—diagonally in one direction and diagonally in another direction create interesting features and sections within the overall basket design.

In this design, Lynette used predominantly chain stitch to complete the design with vertical satin stitch to emphasize a border at the top and bottom of the basket. Satin stitch has been completed in a vertical manner with stitches very close to one other.

Lynette made this basket design into a purse, with matching African fabric surrounding it.

The Xhosa Tribe

The Xhosa tribe is the tribe from which Nelson Mandela is descended.

Xhosa people have made their homes in the Eastern and Western Cape. They are well known for painting their faces, their blankets, pipes and chest-beating dances. In Xhosa villages, individual homes are built in the shape of conical roofed huts with mud walls.

The inside of the huts is smeared with cow dung and traditionally men sit to the left and women to the right of the fireplace.

Corn, also known as maize or "mielies," is crushed in a hole in the middle of the group. Crushed corn is used to make a staple meal called "pap."

Here I am standing next to a Zulu women carrying a pot on her head, on a recent trip to South Africa

Standing outside a traditional Ndebele house which has been hand painted using bright colors.

African Masks

Masks have been a part of African tradition and tribal custom for many years. Masks have played a major role in rituals, celebrations, ceremonial and tribal initiations. Masking rituals are normally accompanied with prayer, music, song and/or dance. Traditionally song and dance will accompany the wearing of masks in ceremonies or festivities for the entire village. At certain times, masks can be worn as symbols of power to ward off evil spirits, or as a display of gratitude for and thanks to ancestors for rain and a good harvest.

The mask designs displayed in this book have all been completed in different ways. Blanch Jones' mask design on the right is completed using chain stitch, satin stitch and French knots on either side of the

face. Only the actual lines of the drawing have been embroidered upon.

As opposed to my mask design on the left, where the sides of the face have been completed and filled in using satin stitch, and the borders on either side have been completed using fabric and trim hand-stitched directly onto the design. A beaded Zulu bracelet and Zulu pin have been stitched above the face of the mask. My mask has then been quilted and converted into a wall hanging, while Blanch's mask has been framed, showing the different applications and uses for African Folklore Embroidery designs.

Analee Perica, who completed both of the masks below, used different techniques and creative inspiration for each of the designs. Analee's beautiful stitches and fine handiwork give the impression that the stitched parts of the design have been painted onto the fabric. Her use of very fine threads and small, tight chain stitch assist in creating this effect. Analee converted each of the mask designs into wearable art vests, one for herself and one for her husband.

Other Animals You Can Expect to See in South Africa

Crocodiles, Lizards and Tortoises

Our safari now takes us back into the African bushveld. Crocodiles can be found in Gauteng and on the KwaZulu-Natal coast on crocodile farms. The Nile crocodile, known as a large, lizard-shaped reptile with four short legs and a long muscular tail, is found throughout Africa. With their rough, scaly hide the crocodile can weigh approximately 2,500lbs. Crocs, as they are affectionately known, enjoy eating fish, buck, hippos, zebra and porcupines. Males can extend up to ten feet in length. A female crocodile can lay 25 to 100 eggs, which she covers with sand, then guards until they hatch three months later. When young crocodiles are hatching, either parent may help them out of the egg by rolling it between their tongue and palate. This cracks the shell, allowing for an easier escape. The average life span of a crocodile is about forty-five years.

The first example of the crocodile (AN18)shows the wonderful usage of satin stitch. All the inner smaller circles and some of the triangles have been filled in using satin stitch, giving a smooth, satiny appearance. This completed crocodile has been made into a table mat.

The crocodile on the right, completed by Robin Roberts, makes use of African hand-dyed variegated threads to fill in with the satin stitch. Forest (54) with over ten different shades of green is wonderful to use for satin stitch and filling in small areas. Further filling in areas with some short satin stitch and then some long satin stitch and then short satin stitch in a pattern has great effect when using the variegated thread color Forest (54).

Connie Anderson used chain stitch to complete this design, using many different solid colors, sometimes outlining using one solid color and then filling the inside in chain stitch with a different solid color. The circles on the body of the crocodile have become features within the design, being completed and filled in using chain stitch.

Lizards

Spending time in Durban, in the KwaZulu-Natal province, is a culturally enriching experience. Durban's tropical climate, humidity and rain in summer and beautiful warm winters make it an ideal place for lizards to thrive and multiply. My husband grew up in Durban and my in-laws and husband's family still live there. Visits to my in-laws involve frequent encounters with lizards climbing up and down walls. South Africa is the ideal destination for an African "herping" safari. It is home to a unique and diverse array of reptiles and amphibians, including a variety of snakes, lizards, worm lizards, crocodiles, tortoises, turtles and frogs Besides tortoises, lizards are most easily seen and on sunny days may often be spied basking on rocky outcrops. In South Africa there is approximately the same number of reptile species as mammal species. The lizard design below has been completed using chain stitch,

variegated color, metallic and solid threads. It has then been quilted using a selection of African fabrics.

Taking the lizard design to the next level, Connie Anderson not only beautifully embroidered the lizard design on the left, she then embroidered a second lizard design and cut out each individual lizard and stitched it onto this quilt she made.

Stitched, pieced and quilted by Sharon Camping and Billie's Stitching Post

Tortoises

Now here is an interesting tidbit of information. Did you know that tortoises urinate as a means of defense, so it is best not to pick them up as this will deplete their limited water supply?

Africa has the richest tortoise diversity of any place on earth. Some of these species, such as the endangered Geometric tortoise, are rarely encountered, but others, such as the Angulate, Leopard and Hinge-back tortoises are commonly maintained in captive collections within South Africa.

Jennifer and Darlene Solotkin have several large tortoises living in their home, so when they saw this design, they were most excited to get started. They used gold metallic threads for the leaves in their tortoise design and stitched on beads for the outline of the circles on the tortoise's body.

Sharon Camping used hand-dyed variegated browns—Cloves (55), Fern

(4) and Bush (8)—to complete this tortoise, as well as the Mola Barbara Interweaving Technique on the head of the tortoise. Sharon quilted the completed design with fabric that picked up the tones and shades used to embroider the tortoise.

I had such fun completing my tortoise using chain stitch and colorful solid thread colors.

Once complete, I hand-stitched black, pink, green and purple trim around the edges and stitched the whole design onto the back of a denim jacket!

Monkeys

Our safari now takes us to the picturesque South African coastline of KwaZulu-Natal, where troops of monkeys have made their home. Maybe it's all those easily accessible bananas that grow so well in the Durban climate that has made the monkey population in Durban thrive and increase. You can expect to see monkeys in Cape Town at Chapman's Peak (where the Atlantic and Indian Ocean meet) and outside of Johannesburg near Sun City and the Pilanesberg Game reserve. Monkeys in these areas are not caged but roam freely.

They like swinging from tees, climbing onto rooftops, and climbing on top of cars. They often hang out with their families, the babies clutching onto the bottom of their mothers tummies as they run, walk and climb. They are very cute to observe, however it is strongly suggested that you do not pat or feed them human food. Sometimes if you are too close to a family of monkeys they may feel threatened and misinterpret your gestures. Monkeys will let you know how they feel. If a male monkey does not want you coming close to him or his troop or taking photographs, he will begin flailing his arms and hissing. Since this happened to us on a trip to South Africa, we learnt from my father-in-law that you never turn your back on an angry monkey; rather walk backwards imitating their movements.

One of the most commonly seen monkeys in Africa is the vervet monkey, also known as the green monkey, which is fearless and assertive. Perhaps because of the climate and lush vegetation in Durban, monkeys abound. From my in-laws' house you can see monkeys, and when we go down to the north coast to San Lameer—one of my favorite places in South Africa—we stay inside a monkey reserve. Frequently we will wake up to find monkeys on the roof, on the patio, and swinging from branches outside. As long as you do not try to feed the monkeys or bother them and their babies, they are quite content to let you observe them. I love observing their mischievous behavior and often human-like manner. However, be warned if you are near monkeys, do not leave your bags or food unattended, as they are inclined to snatch, grab and "steal" things that do not belong to them!

While many local inhabitants enjoy living side-by-side with the monkeys, others complain that they make it challenging to grow fruit and vegetables because they devour the crops before they can be harvested. Some are sent to a private sanctuary 320 kilometers outside Durban, where they are kept until they can be released into the bush. In San Lameer, a bird haven with golf courses and parks, monkeys flourish and raise their young.

I have always loved monkeys; in fact growing up my grandmother, Sally, had a monkey named Chiquita as a pet. Chiquita was extremely mischievous. In this monkey design I used different shades of variegated brown threads such as Coppertone (37) and Forest (54) with chain stitch interspersed with French knots on the body of the monkey.

Sharon Camping used a technique called needle-felting on the design on the left, where she fused brown velvety fabric onto the body of the monkeys.

Using variegated color Freesia (48), she chain-stitched the trunk of the tree and completed the leaves using Holly (56).

Birds

With over 3,000 bird species living in South Africa, it is the ideal destination for bird lovers. While many of the bird designs are of a folkloric nature, the largest population of ostriches in the world can be found in a tiny city in South Africa called Oudtshoorn. The ostrich is the largest living bird on earth. Few people can say they've ridden on an ostrich! In South Africa, if you dare, you can ride an ostrich in one of the more than 400 ostrich farms. The ostrich industry sells and promotes their ostrich meat, ostrich leather, ostrich eggs and general tourism. Ostrich eggs ornately decorated and painted are collectable items and are displayed in people's home as ornaments.

When fully grown an ostrich weighs over 240lbs. The male ostrich is easy to recognize with soft black feathers on its back and white feathers on its wings and tail. Females and young ostriches have brown feathers instead of black to camouflage them. Both males and females have bare necks and thighs. Ostriches are distinguishable by their long necks, small heads, large eyes, long, powerful legs, and two toes on each foot. One ostrich egg is equivalent to sixteen regular eggs. That's quite an omelet you can make!

In the ostrich design on the left, completed by Connie Anderson, she makes use of sequins in the body of the ostrich and strings of green beads and chain stitch for the tail. Tiny clusters of gold beads can be found on the claws of the bird. Beads have been used for the rays of the sun and serve to emphasize and accentuate the inner circle of the sun.

This ostrich design above was completed in muted colors by Sally Fasteau. This is one of the first examples I have seen of using a selection of variegated browns and grays on the black fabric for a beautiful contrast.

She used chain stitch to border the circles and then filled them in with satin stitch in the same color as the outer chain stitch border. Each strand of the ostrich's tail has been stitched in a different shade of brown.

The completed design was converted by Sally into a pillow.

Lia Smith completed this ostrich design using bright solid colors. For the tail, the Mola Barbara Interweaving Technique has been done on top of the chain stitch.

African Folkloric Bird Designs

The beak bird design (B14) is embroidered using a wide selection of variegated threads including colors Flame (43) and Autumn (13). A tiny chain stitch has been used for the outlines, with the middle of the bird's body being completed in a blanket stitch.

What makes the tail interesting, specifically the feathers, is the integration of tiny vertical and horizontal chain stitch. On each side of the vertical chain stitch is embellishment; to the left little French knots in solid yellow, and to the right a string of clear-colored beads.

The beak of the bird has been filled in using tight, small chain stitch. Sequins and beads have been stitched in the body of the bird.

My favorite part of the hairy bird design (B13) is its beak which has been filled in using a smooth satin stitch with a variegated thread color called Flame (43). The outline of the beak has been embroidered using a satin-type stitch in gold metallic, size 8. The body of the bird is particularly interesting as the circles have been outlined in a variegated chain stitch and filled in using a solid color and satin stitch. Blanket stitch has been used for the body of the snail. The bottom part of the tail has been embellished in a very subtle manner. Between each of the solid chain stitch lines, cross stitch has been done; wherever the stitches meet, touch or cross, those areas have been couched in a different colored thread to the cross stitch.

The use of so many different colors along with the subtle yet slightly varied embellishment of each part of this bird is what makes it so interesting and spectacular. Viewing the upper feathers of the bird, chain stitch has been used for the outline, blanket stitch for filling in the sides, and cross stitch and couching in gold metallic is how the rest of the area is filled in. The tail again makes use of a tightly woven chain stitch and blanket stitch with the middle of this section using the cross stitch techniques and couching the interconnecting threads with metallic gold thread. There are hints of metallic gold used throughout this design and they each subtly pick up on each other.

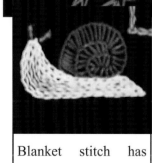

Blanket stitch has been used for the body of the snail.

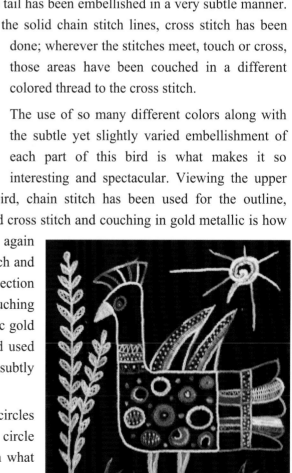

Remember, just because you decide to fill in one of the circles on the body with only chain stitch, it does not imply that every circle needs to be completed in the same way—the difference is often what creates the contrast and uniqueness of the design.

Also known as the bird with attitude, (B15) Each part of this bird has become a feature within itself. Let's start with the beak where a similar technique has been used as with the hairy bird's beak. The tail has been stitched using chain stitch for the lines and in between the lines it has been filled in with cross stitch. Where threads interconnect couching is done in a different color thread, creating a contrast. The circles on the bird's body have been filled in using a solid blue thread in back stitch and the middle filled in using satin stitch with variegated color Freesia (48).

The middle part of the bird perhaps looks the most intricate, however nothing with African Folklore Embroidery is ever really complicated or difficult when broken down and explained in steps. A straight stitch in yellows and blues has been stitched in a vertical manner, small French knots separate the groups of satin stitch from one other, and hints of metallic are interspersed with the satin stitch. The fattest part of the bird's body incorporates the criss-cross couching technique along with chain stitch. The slightly raised and lumpy part of this section is tightly wound bullion stitch using variegated thread Viola (14) in a vertical manner. Variegated color Forest (54) has been used for the leaves. The eye of the bird has been completed with the outer area in back stitch and the bottom area filled in a vertical satin stitch.

To the right is the fat kuku bird (B15) as he appeared in the Summer 2006 issue of *Fons & Porter's Love of Quilting*. For this design, I did the embroidery and *Fons & Porter's Love of Quilting* did the quilting. Beads from Embellishment Village were stitched into the quilt for enhancement.

Connie Anderson completed each of these bird designs. Both Connie's stitches and her combination of colors are true art. In B10 on the left, Connie used beads and the criss-cross technique to enhance the bird. Clusters of beads surrounded by chain stitch are on the bird's body, and beads in between the sun's rays accentuate the yellow of the sun. Connie used solid, bright colors for this design. The simplicity of the green chain-stitched leaves on the side of the bird contrasts and offsets the bright colors of the bird.

In B13 on the right, Connie used beads and sequins in the hair of the bird. She also incorporated sequins onto the body of the hairy bird and bordered the sequins with chain stitch, making them "pop" out and be even more effective. The sun in this design has been made into a feature using gold and brass elongated beads between the sun's rays.

The eye of the bird has been constructed by placing a bead on top of a sequin which gives the bird "character"—and an almost obnoxious expression! Sprinkles of tiny pink and orange beads have been interspersed with chain stitch on the neck of the bird. The outlines of the leaves are chain stitch.

Design B14, the bird with a beak, can be interpreted in so many different ways. In the design on the left, completed by Sharon Camping and Heidi Monaly, the bird's beak has been filled in with yellow chain stitch and each of her leaves has been completed using a different color.

The design on the right, completed by Jonda Fredel and Charlotte Jokinan, the sun has been stitched using the Mola Barbara Interweaving Technique. Satin stitch is used as an embellishment technique to fill in parts of the bird's body.

This is one of our most well-known designs, the fat bird, also known as the bird with attitude. These two designs have been completed in their own unique way by Sharon Camping and Connie Anderson.

These bird designs have been made into quilts. Chardel Blaine quilted her birds with bright yellow fabric and a black and colored border.

Each of the leaves on the guitar tree in design B20 has been completed in a different variegated color using blanket stitch. The outline of the birds' bodies has been completed in chain stitch using Freesia (48). The second design (B18) uses chain stitch in bright, solid colors.

Peacocks

Yes, you can expect to see beautiful peacocks in South Africa, especially at Mitchell Botanical Gardens in Durban and The World of Birds in Cape Town. The peacock design (B16) can be viewed by some as more challenging. But in truth, the stitches are the same as one would use for any of the African Folklore Embroidery designs and the decision to approach the design with symmetry (the same colors on either side of the tail) is personal. In the following pages we showcase some completed peacock designs. Each is unique and beautiful.

Using only chain stitch and some beads, Pam Ross completed the peacock above. The elegance, neatness and tightness of this chain stitch, together with the consistency of the colors used in each feather, make for an extraordinary piece of art.

Darlene and Jennifer Solotkin used turquoise sequins for the inside of each feather, creating a dazzling effect. The outlines of the leaves are completed in back stitch using Freesia (48). This design has been converted into a bag.

Denise Engel completed the peacock design on the right using metallic threads and solid pink and blues to do the chain stitch.

The peacock below, completed by Una Yvonne uses blanket stitch to outline each of the feathers, while the body of the peacock is completed in satin stitch, using variegated shades of green, yellow and brown.

This peacock design was completed by Robbie Eben using chain stitch. Robbie's stitches are so even and smooth that it looks like the design has been painted.

Butterflies (AN20)

Ever been on a butterfly safari? Well, a trip to Cape Town's Butterfly World will open your eyes to a whole other beautiful side of South Africa. You can expect to see the most beautiful butterflies in South Africa.

I so enjoyed completing this design and incorporating different mediums. This butterfly design is a true fiber art project, combining threads, fibers (look at the pink yarn in the middle of the pink butterfly, scraps of fabric appliquéd into the design, sequins and beads). Metallic threads, silk ribbon and stranded floss have also been incorporated to create true fabric-fiber-beading fusion.

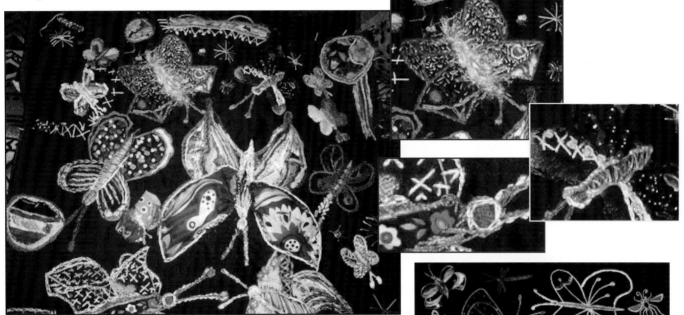

This butterfly design was completed by my mom, Barbara, while we were on a family stitching retreat, makes use of small seed beads for spots on the red butterfly and variegated threads for enhancement and accent. Only the outlines of the butterflies have been stitched and on the inside of the designs the black spaces are easily seen, creating a contrast between the colors and the background fabric.

My cousin, Lynette Hasson, embroidered this butterfly design (while on our family vacation) and turned it into an evening purse. She used muted variegated shades of light pinks, greens and blues.

51

Flora and Fauna of South Africa

Are you feeling a little tired, ready for some refreshments on our safari? How about a cup of tea and English scones in the famous Kirstenbosch Botanical Gardens on the eastern slopes of Table Mountain? My sister, Michele, and brother, David, and I spent many Sunday afternoons playing and running around on the green grass and smelling the flowers at Kirstenbosch. Here you can see about 6,000 floral species and more than 22,000 indigenous plants—particularly those of the Cape floral kingdom, known as *fynbos*.

The protea is the national flower of South Africa and is found throughout the country. The famous Protea

Garden with a large variety of protea species is inside Kirstenbosch. There are 370 protea species found in South Africa. The King Protea has flower heads up to 10 inches across, with widely spaced bracts arranged around a peak of flowers that vary in color from near white to soft silvery-pink to deep rose pink or crimson. Many of the African Folklore Embroidery designs feature different protea species, some closed and others open.

Small, tight chain stitch has been used to complete this protea design (FL11), which displays both closed and open protea. A combination of variegated pinks, such as Camellia (35) and Rose (16) has been used to achieve the various shades of pink seen in the protea flower.

In design AN25 on the left, the dragonflies and flower have been completed in hand-dyed variegated thread colors Peacock (38), Flame (32), Maple (65) and Camellia (35).

The outline of the pink flowers has been completed in blanket stitch. The dragonfly has been stitched using gold metallic thread. The inside of the flowers to the right have been filled in with Flame (32) in satin stitch.

A criss-cross stitch has been used for the inside of the leaves on the right-hand side. Small beads have been stitched on to the design for the eye of the bugs and parts of the flowers. The use of satin stitch creates a smoothness and almost "painted" look to some of the flowers.

The dragonfly has been stitched using gold metallic thread.

The inside of the flowers has been filled in with Flame (32) in satin stitch.

The design FL18 on the left, incorporates tightly woven chain stitch for most of the elements, except for blanket stitch for the body of the snail and satin stitch for the body of the caterpillar and the spider has been completed in Clementis (63)

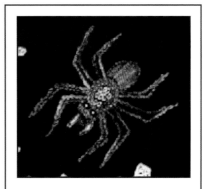

The spider has been completed in one of my favorite variegated colors, Clementis (63)

In design FL19 (below), the two flowers on the upper right-hand side are completed using tight bullion stitch in Freesia (48) and Vernon (87).

Gold beads have been stitched onto part of the bag. Satin stitch was used to fill in part of the leaves and flowers. I love how much detail there is on this design, with each part of the design becoming a feature within itself. Starting on the top left-hand side, round gold beads have been stitched onto the stems.

These same beads have been stitched onto the stems on the bottom right-hand side, creating a balance. A significant amount of satin stitch has been used throughout the design. Freesia (48) and Cabbage (30) are the main variegated colors that have been incorporated into the design.

The use of bullion stitch and variegated threads creates an interesting three-dimensional effect. Certain flowers have been given a second outline in chain stitch, with the result being an emphasis on the borders of those particular elements within the design. The cluster of beads in the middle of the flowers helps to draw the eye to that area.

The cluster of beads draws attention to the center of the flower

Gold beads have been added to the leaves.

South African Marine Life

If you are feeling hot from time spent outside while on safari, and in need of some time at the beach to cool off, Boulders Beach is the perfect place. It is also one of my favorite places to spend time while in South Africa, swimming and frolicking with penguins. Located in Simon's Town (about twenty minutes drive from Cape Town), Boulders Beach is home to a colony of more than 2,500 **African Penguins** (also known as the Jackass Penguin), and is the only place in the world where one can actually swim amongst the penguins.

These African Penguins are tame and comfortable with humans. They can be seen playing and sunning themselves in between people sunbathing and swimming on the beach. They are not bothered or scared of people, however one should avoid harassing them by getting too close or chasing them. Beware!! They can bite. They are happy to be quietly observed from a close distance.

Penguins cannot fly, however they are excellent divers and can remain underwater for up to twenty minutes! While there are many species of penguins, the African Penguin is the only one to inhabit the African continent.

African Penguins can be recognized by a black stripe curving across the top of the chest. They are known to be clumsy on land, however in the sea they are extremely skillful and graceful swimmers and can swim up to fifteen miles per hour.

Lori Russell did a superb job stitching the mermaid design (OC 15) on the left and then making it into a quilt using ocean fabrics. Lori used chain stitch, solid and variegated threads and beads to complete this design. Please note this is a folkloric designs, you will not see mermaids in South Africa!

I love the crispness of design B17. The emphasis is on the outlines of the dolphins and birds using chain stitch and variegated colors, Freesia (48), Clementis (63) and Vernon (87). Only the inside part of the penguin's body has been filled in with white chain stitch.

African Penguins inhabit twenty-seven sites in Africa. Most are on inshore islands, of which the best known is Robben Island, along the South African coastline. Three of the other main penguin sites in South Africa include the largest existing colony on St. Croix island near Port Elizabeth, with about 50,000 birds. Dassen Island off Yzerfontein, once home to over a million penguins, now has about 30,000, while Dyer Island near Gansbaai has about 20,000.

African Penguins feed mainly on small pelagic fish (fish which swim on the upper layers of the open ocean) like pilchards, anchovies, horse mackerel and herrings. Competition with commercial fishing has forced them to adapt their diet. They also eat squid and small crustaceans. Male penguins are slightly larger than female penguins. Penguins are usually about four years old when they begin breeding. African Penguins will remain with a single partner for many years, producing one or two eggs a year. The Boulders Beach penguin population tends to breed in March to May. The incubation period lasts 40 days, and the fledging period from 60 to 130 days.

The penguins nest in crude shallow burrows dug out of the sand or under beach vegetation. The main reason for digging burrows is to protect the eggs and chicks from the heat of the sun. Penguins prefer to return to the same nesting site each year.

When the babies hatch, they are already covered in a layer of gray, fluffy feathers which provide them with insulation and waterproofing. The parents share the nesting and feeding duties. While one partner stays behind, without food or water, for about two-and- a-half days, the hunting partner will swim as much as ten miles out to sea to find tasty food. The babies are usually fed in the late afternoon. The parents regurgitate partially digested fish into their mouths. Parents continue to keep close watch on their chicks for about a month and the chicks leave the nest after about two months. Having been there around the time when the eggs are hatching it is really cute to see these baby penguins.

In design OC11 on the right, metallic threads have been used to enhance the design. Small tight chain stitch and hand-dyed variegated colors, Freesia (48) and Vernon (87), give the design accent. Small beads have been incorporated into the design.

Using solid colors for the body of the fish and variegated color Forest (54) for the ocean line, Connie Anderson created a work of art with her fish design (OC10) on the right.

In design OC11 above left, "Under the Sea," Connie used a combination of metallic threads, beads and variegated colors to enhance the design.

This design was Jennifer Solotkin's first attempt at stitching. Her inspiration was the story of the "Rainbow fish." She added her own uniqueness to the design, by adding in eyebrows.

Angie Polopsian used bright, solid colors and chain stitch to complete the design below—"Under the Sea."

The British Influence on South Africa

In the 1800s South Africa was a British colony. As a result many of the British traditions, such as tea drinking, were adopted by local South Africans. Today tea is an everyday, sometimes twice a day, ritual with tea being drunk in the mornings at eleven and in the afternoon at four. Tea is generally drunk from a teacup and saucer. The teapot and teacup designs reflect the British influence on everyday South African life.

The teapot designs with animals (AF28) and flowers (AF30) reflect the different styles and colors for completing the teapot design. While you view these pages, be sure to make yourself a cup of tea.

Heidi Monaly chain-stitched her teapot on the left using a combination of solid blues, greens, purples, oranges and yellows..

I used variegated colors Freesia (48) and Forest (54) to complete my teapot. I have since had it framed and gave it to my sister, Michele, for her birthday. Michele is an avid tea drinker.

Embroidering with the chain stitch, Raya Kaufman used light and bright colors for the teapot on the right.

All of the teacup designs below were embroidered by my highly talented and creative cousin, Lynette Hasson. In each design Lynette makes use of African hand-dyed variegated threads.

In design QB18 she used Peacock (38), Brass (47), Berry (20) and Freesia (48) for the butterfly. In QB17, Forget-me-not (21), Maple (65), The Sea (36) and Brass (47) have been used. Chain stitch is the dominant stitch used to complete these teacups.

Lynette used French knots, chain stitch and criss-cross stitch to embroider design QB20. The use of satin stitch using variegated color Fern (4) accentuates the top and bottom of the teacup.

Analee Perica used bright, solid colors to complete the design on the left in chain stitch. She outlined the teapot in gold metallic thread.

Teaching the Next Generation a Love of Stitching and Ethnic Art

I love teaching kids African Folklore Embroidery. I get a huge sense of pride and delight in seeing how these children, who have never held or threaded a needle, let alone stitched before, after a few lessons, become enthusiastic and accomplished stitchers in satin and chain stitch, are able to thread their own needles, tie knots and add on beads. These important life skills will be taken and become part of these children for the rest of their lives. Like riding a bike, learning how to do these stitches is something they will never forget. I have found that when you teach boys and girls under the age of twelve to stitch there is no gender stigma; in fact both boys and girls love the fact that they can choose whichever color they wish to stitch and are not restricted by color choice. In fact it is the lack of rules and freedom of choice with colors and authenticity that engages children in African Folklore Embroidery. Many adults were discouraged when they first started stitching by a belief that stitches had to be "perfect." African Folklore Embroidery steers away from this approach and in fact promotes the belief that there are "no needle art police who are going to come and inspect stitches and the back of an embroidery design."

In the past few years I have taught thousands of children the art of African Folklore Embroidery at girl scout troops, in-school and after school enrichment programs, summer camps and birthday parties. Any lesson starts with an explanation of the rules relating to African Folklore Embroidery. When we start teaching children to stitch I suggest double-threading the needle. That way there is none of the frustration if the needle becomes unthreaded.

African Folklore Embroidery is a colorful, fun, creative needlecraft for boys and girls seven years and older.

While strengthening hand-eye coordination and fine motor skills, it also allows students to be creative, use their imaginations and learn about African wildlife and culture. Below are some comments from educators, parents and children regarding African Folklore Embroidery:

"The fourth and fifth graders at our school really enjoyed the African Folklore Embroidery class we offered through our after-school art program...Boys and girls alike were engaged in this peaceful artistic process and became quite knowledgeable about the Ndebele tribe at the same time. After we showcased some of their beautiful work at our school art festival, parents and staff signed up for classes as well!"—

Amanda, 8

Gayle Nadler, Public Relations and Grant Manager for the Multicultural Learning Center Charter School, Canoga Park, CA

Summer Art Camp

"My son and daughter both enjoy doing African Folklore Embroidery. I like having them do it because it improves their hand-eye coordination. They will also see the results of their efforts very quickly unlike other types of needlework."— Susan, Woodland Hills, CA

"My daughter learned how to do African Folklore Embroidery at camp. I loved watching her do it. She was so excited about what she was creating, she wanted to show me how to do it and now we do it together. It has become our special project. We both work on our kit designs together and talk."—Stephanie, Calabasas, CA

"I like African Folklore Embroidery because it is very relaxing and fun. You get to learn chain stitch. It is cool because you get to express yourself and nothing has to be the color it is in real life. The Ndebele tribe is cool. The women are famous for their beadwork. But the main reason I like African Folklore Embroidery is because it is fun." —Victoria, 8, Santa Monica, CA

"I like doing the chain stitch; it is cool."—Josh, 8, Woodland Hills, CA

"I like African Folklore Embroidery because you get to choose whatever color you want to stitch. I also think

embroidery is fascinating because you just do a few simple things and it comes out so nicely."—Alex, CA

"African Folklore Embroidery is different from regular sewing. It is very relaxing to do. It keeps your interest and has a wonderful outcome. You don't have to stay true to real colors so you can make anything any color you want. I would love it if they offered this at my school."—Rebecca, 10, Los Angeles, CA

"My favorite thing in the whole world to do is African Folklore Embroidery. The chain stitch is really easy to do. My brother likes doing it too."—Vital, 8, Encino, CA

Girl scouts earn badges and points toward badges with African Folklore Embroidery multi cultural stitching sessions. With different programs for Daisy's Brownie, Junior and Senior Cadettes, girl scouts can each take a

visual safari to South Africa through various embroidery techniques, African artifacts and beading. Workshops are either conducted by an African Folklore Embroidery Educator or teaching material is sent to troop leaders. The educational programs allow for troops to experience Africa by learning about the history and culture of the Ndebele tribe through African Folklore Embroidery.

Using colorful African threads and beads against a black background, students embroider images of Ndebele life as they learn about the lifestyle and customs of this fascinating culture and community.

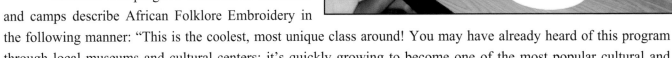

Teachers and program directors at museums and camps describe African Folklore Embroidery in the following manner: "This is the coolest, most unique class around! You may have already heard of this program through local museums and cultural centers; it's quickly growing to become one of the most popular cultural and artistic courses available. The beauty of African Folklore Embroidery lies in its simplicity and individuality. The extreme contrasts of brightly colored threads against the black fabric make any completed design both striking and beautiful. The designs taught can be completed in basic chain stitch or elaborately, with the addition of beads, sequins and the use of variegated and metallic threads.

"I like African Folklore Embroidery because when you do the chain stitch it looks really pretty."—Alexandra, 9, Calabasas, CA

"I like African Folklore Embroidery because it is really fun and the designs are beautiful."—Fiona, 9, Sherman Oaks, CA

"African Folklore Embroidery is cool because you learn about tribes far away in South Africa. I love the beautiful colors of the threads. I like learning the chain stitch."—Stella 10, Studio City, CA

"I like African Folklore Embroidery because you can find a design you like and choose your own colors. You can make it your own with

different types of threads and colors. It is also part of a rich culture that we are getting to learn about."—Sarah, 12, Calabasas, CA

" I love to sew and I love South Africa. I am enjoying this class so much. I really hope to do this again soon at my school."—Ariana, 9, Los Angeles, CA

When I see how excited children get from learning a new skill and then going home and teaching their moms to stitch, I really get excited. There is a whole generation of

women who have never held needles before, never stitched a stitch or beaded a button; reaching out to this group of people has been particularly rewarding, especially to those women who perhaps always felt, *Oh, needle art is not for me.* When they see how easy and how relaxing it is, and yes even when one is so busy running around with one's kids and school and after-school activities, there are so many times in the day, just waiting and passing time, that can be used to relax, switch off and do the African Folklore Embroidery. I wanted to share some comments from some of these women.

"I just returned from a trip to Ireland to visit my brother and his girlfriend. Needless to say, I brought my African Folklore Embroidery along the way. My brother's girlfriend, who is in her mid-twenties, very "hip" with style, a love for art, creative, artistic and a love for the eclectic, and as it turned out, very accomplished in cross stitch and knitting, took a liking to it when I showed it to her. I hadn't had a chance to get to know her very well before this trip and didn't think I, a 37-year-old mom of two, would have much in common with her. Your kits and thread turned out to be the "thread" that connected us. I showed her the website, told her about the background, and offered her the large animal design I had brought along, but hadn't started. At first she turned it down, saying she would look at the website and pick one later. I let her try some stitches on mine. The next day she asked if she could, after all, take that one. She started it immediately and she and I have many moments of sitting and sewing together. I thought you would enjoy this story!"—Melanie

"I loved doing the "Under the Sea" design. All the sea creatures were so interesting and I could make it as colorful as I wanted. African Folklore Embroidery is like an escape for me. I can come home from a stressful day at work, start doing my embroidery and forget all about my day. I like learning new stitches and incorporating them into my designs."—Jennifer

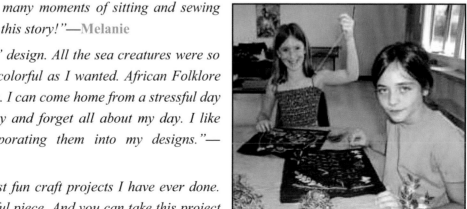

"This is one of the easiest and most fun craft projects I have ever done. Even the novice can make a beautiful piece. And you can take this project anywhere: long car trips, plane rides, mother-in-law's homes! Whether you make this for yourself or give it as a gift you will have a beautiful heirloom."—Alyssa, Sherman Oaks, CA

"I love handiwork of every kind. African Folklore Embroidery gives me peace of mind. It is very relaxing to do. I do it during my lunch hour or in the evening. I have completed six kit designs. I think the turtle was my favorite to do. I

Alexa's first design at age 9

love turtles. I have four turtles at home and so embroidering the turtle design was so much fun. The Noah's Ark design was incredible to do. I loved being able to add all the colorful variegated threads."— Darlene, Chatsworth, CA

"African Folklore Embroidery allows me to be creative and relax all at the same time."—Minette, Calabasas, CA

"My husband never imagined that I would ever get into something like African Folklore Embroidery. I had never done any type of needlework before this. I am totally hooked and cannot put it down!"— Erin, Simi Valley, CA

"I really enjoy African Folklore Embroidery because the scenes are so simplistic that I can be creative without spoiling the design. African Folklore Embroidery is so easy and fun to do. In no time at all it's time for my own unique finishing touches. African Folklore Embroidery is so much fun that it takes my mind off the fact that I'm hungry."—Taffy, Village Glen, CA

" Take a trip to Africa in your classroom and emerge with brightly colored artwork as your prize" Leora Raikin has brought the popularity of African Folklore Embroidery to the attention of scout programs, camps and even homes." **Lori Prentice, *Winning in Education,* August/September 2003**

"African embroidery classes teach needlework and cultural lessons." **Los Angeles, Times, Sept 2003**

"Leaving Children in stitches, African embroidery classes teach needlework and cultural lessons." **Carolyn Patricia Scott, *Los Angeles Times,* September 2003**

Leora Raikin, a native of Cape Town, South Africa, who lives in Los Angeles, has a passion and she wants that passion to spread across the United States-all the way to Maine . Her passion is teaching African Folklore Embroidery and the Ndebele culture of South Africa ." **Ardena Hamlin, *Bangor Daily News, Maine ,* May 2004**

Spreading the Passion—Mentoring, Teaching, Educating

It is almost four years since I started teaching African Folklore Embroidery to adults and children across the United States. Since then 6,000 people have completed an African Folklore Embroidery class. It has been so exciting to see the response from quilters, embroiderers and those who have never stitched before and are stunned by their results! I get so excited and proud when my students email me pictures of their completed designs.

In order to keep up with the growing requests for lectures, workshops and classes throughout the United States and Canada, and continue with our mission to educate people about South Africa through African Folklore Embroidery, I developed the **African Folklore Embroidery Educators Training Program.** Through training and educational material this allows for others to lecture and teach African Folklore Embroidery at guilds, shops, museums, scout troops and summer camps.

In the lectures I present on African Folklore Embroidery I try and convey information about South Africa and African Folklore Embroidery in a humorous, entertaining, informative and interactive manner. A percentage of my lecture fee is donated to Kidzpositive, an AIDS charity that supports mothers and children with AIDS in South Africa. Through Kidzpositve, mothers are trained to make and produce beaded items for sale, allowing mothers with AIDS the opportunity to support their family and regain a sense of dignity and pride. These moms have been taught to use a bead-loom to create beaded pens, beaded flags, beaded key rings and beaded bookmarks. Designs on each item can be customized to suit customers' or company's names or information.

Kidzpositive currently supports 130 families with a regular weekly income. Mothers are further provided with training and the raw materials to produce beadwork in their own homes. Kidzpositive generates hope, skills and funds with a positive attitude toward mothers and children living with HIV/AIDS. The success of this project constantly requires new orders. Kidzpositive is located at Groote Schuur Hospital, Cape Town, and they recently established a school for moms wishing to complete high school as well as for children too sick to attend public school.

Workshops

Six-hour workshop (full day): Students will be given a choice of ten different basic kit designs from which to choose (see www.aflembroidery.com). They can either choose before or at the class. Kits include design, needle, braid of brightly colored threads, stitch diagram and beads. This workshop includes the following:

History and background of African Folklore Embroidery

Culture, traditions and customs of the Ndebele tribe

Learn the stitching techniques for completing an African Folklore Embroidery design

    a. Chain stitch - b. Satin stitch - c. French knots - d. Bullion stitch

Embellishment techniques for enhancement and effects

    a. Use of color and variegated threads - b. Use of metallic thread

    c. Beading and beadwork techniques

Playing with threads and color

Mixing threads and fibers

Enhancement and visual art techniques

Fabric-Fiber Fusion (6 hours)

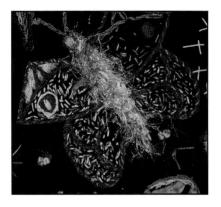

Learn all the techniques from the workshop, plus creating fiber art out of African Folklore Embroidery; cutting and stitching of different fabric onto the design.

Lecture, Exhibition & Trunk Show

One-hour lecture, exhibition, sample displays and interactive discussion on the Ndebele tribe, African wildlife and techniques used for completing an African Folklore Embroidery design. African Folklore Embroidery kits and African hand-dyed threads and Ndebele hand-beaded dolls are available for sale after the lecture. Pop quiz (with hand-dyed African threads as prizes) included in the lecture.

The only material needed for all workshops is a pair of scissors.

All educational materials are provided to educators, however passion, enthusiasm and a love of doing African Folklore Embroidery, a desire to teach and educate about another culture, and encourage a love of color and creativity are key ingredients.

Appliqué the African Way [NEW]

You are going to love our new workshop; it is a creative fusion of quilting, appliqué, embroidery and fiber art all through African Folklore Embroidery, be ready for more fun than you can imagine! (this can be added to the six-hour workshop).

Quilting, Purses, Pillows and Bag Conversion Workshop [NEW]

Okay, now you are complete with your African Folklore Embroidery design, join our team of educators as we show you how to convert your design into a purse, pillow or bag. See your designs come to life and receive a multitude of compliments!

Wearable and Functional Art From African Folklore Embroidery

There are so many different applications and uses for African Folklore Embroidery designs. From converting them into purses and pillows, quilts and wall hangings to stitching them onto jackets and shirts. Every time I exhibit at a quilt show or lecture at a guild, I am so excited to see all the new, creative applications for African Folklore Embroidery by past students. The jacket below was completed by Judy Fisher. I so enjoyed stitching the trim onto the lion design and then onto my black shirt.

Elisa Purnell converted her Ndebele sisters design into a purse.

Alexis Kjelstrom completed the apron above

63

Using bright, colorful fabric, Candy Hartman accentuated her hairy bird (B13) completed design and turned it into the colorful pillow on the right

Pillows are a great way to make African Folklore Embroidery into a functional item that can be displayed, used and admired in the home. French knots instead of beads have been used in the hair, giving the appearance of beads and a slightly raised three-dimensional appearance in the village design on the left. (AF22).

AF23 below was turned into a handbag with a black backing and black strap handles.

Stitched onto the back of a denim jacket, Jonda Fredel and Charlotte Jokinan are continually coming up with new, exciting applications for their African Folklore Embroidery.

The quilt design on the right was completed by Robbie Eben. Each panel is a work of art in itself. Robbie then combined all four panels (B16, AF19, AF11 and B18) and quilted them into this fifty-square-inch quilt. Robbie used both solid colors and variegated African threads. She won an award for this quilt.

Both of the quilts below make use of four basic kit panels.

In the bird quilt, designs B14, B13, B15 and B12 are each embroidered separately using the various stitches and techniques illustrated at the beginning of the book.

In the animal quilt below, each panel represents an animal you can expect to see while on safari in South Africa—Hippo (AN13), Lion (AN14), Rhino (AN12) and Elephant (AN10). Each panel is completed using variegated threads with chain stitch and satin stitch being the dominant stitch. In the lion design, Grape (39) is used to fill in the leaves in satin stitch, and the outline of the lion in chain stitch is done using Mango (24). The four panels have been stitched together to form a quilt wall hanging.

Talented Women

The following designs have been completed by some very talented, creative and inspiring women. Each brings their own set of skills and creative expression to the African Folklore Embroidery design, making it unique. I am constantly inspired by the beautiful work completed by others and get so excited and proud to see each and every design completed. When you work on a design and put in time, there is a part of you that becomes invested and fused within the design. I have been very fortunate to meet and spend time with all the women whose work is displayed below.

AF22 completed by Joanne Bloomfield

Completed by Carol Fitzhugh

AN11, AF23 and AN25 completed by Alexis Kjelstrom

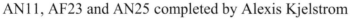

In the design on the right, Connie Anderson, African Folklore Embroidery Educator, Canada, made use of a chain stitch to both outline and fill in the upper body of the fish (OC10) doing the chain stitch in a circular motion, with each circle in a different color. The lower body of the fish has been stitched using open chain stitch and mirrors stitched inside the small circle. The sea line has been depicted with sequins loosely attached above the chain stitch. The top sea line has been depicted with chain stitch and a hint of metallic has been interwoven on top of the chain stitching using the Mola Barbara Interweaving Technique. Connie added a cluster of blue beads on the ocean line to depict a starfish.

The option to do chain stitch horizontally or vertically and the use of chain stitch in both directions in the same design create an interesting effect.

Within the dress of the lady in design AF23, we see the use of vertical chain stitch and in the bottom half of the dress tightly stitched horizontal chain stitch.

Since beads are an integral part of Ndebele dress and culture, a three-layered string of beads has been stitched below the neck. A single bead has been stitched in each of the semi circles above the head.

In design AF25 on the right, Connie incorporates fabrics into the dress and embellishes them with chain and satin stitch.

Analee Perica did a superb job in making her fish (OC10), which she named Chester, come to life. Using small, tight chain

stitch, every part of the design is filled in. The tightness and color of the tail make it into a feature within the design. I love the fabric she chose to complete this design into a purse. The Ndebele village scene above (AF25) has been completed in the same manner with the addition of beads. Analee used chain stitch to fill in the body of the birds.

Analee used the same technique to complete her giraffe. The giraffe's (AN11) complete body has been filled in using different colors of threads with chain stitch.

Sharon Camping and Heidi Monaly won an award for their completed bird quilt design below. The four basic kit bird designs (B14, B12, B15, and B10) have been embroidered using chain stitch, satin stitch and a combination of solid and variegated African threads, and then made into a quilt.

While chain stitch is the dominant stitch used, the choice and variety of the hand-dyed African variegated colors enhance the design.

The peacock design on the right, completed by Sharon Camping uses small chain stitch to fill in all spaces and areas within the design.

The pinks used within the design have been picked up in the quilted fabric. The peacock (B16) has been used as the centerpiece for this quilt.

Carol Chamliss won an award for her completed peacock design. What makes this design so effective is the consistency and symmetry of the chain stitch and the consistency of the colors throughout the peacock's tail. You look at it and you just want to say "WOW!"

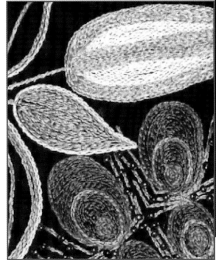

Robin Roberts completed both of these designs using a combination of pearl 8 solid threads and gold metallic size 8. Robin has used predominantly chain stitch to complete the peacock and open chain for the flowers below, with the butterflies being filled in with satin stitch. The two ladies in design AF14 exemplify an extraordinary application of beadwork into African Folklore Embroidery. Robin based her designs on the authentic Ndebele beaded apron. In addition to the intricate beadwork, going in both a vertical and a horizontal direction, she has used small chain stitch and satin stitch for other areas.

B-10

AF-26

Designs B-10, B-14 and AF-26 were completed by sisters Charlotte Jokinen and Jonda Fredel from Minnesota. In the red bird (B10), the outlines of the designs have been completed in small chain stitch with the Mola Barbara Interweaving Technique wrapping the chain-stitched outline. The beak has been completed using hand-dyed and variegated thread color Freesia (48). The satin stitch is smooth and consistent. Using the Mola Barbara Interweaving Technique fuzzy yarn has been used for the head of the bird. In B14, each of the leaves has been completed in satin stitch using variegated colors Freesia (48) and Forest (54). The color changes in these threads are extraordinary. The petals and the legs of the bird have also been completed in satin stitch. Depending on the angle at

which one completes satin stitch—horizontal, vertical or diagonal—it takes on a different effect.

Eldee Norton completed the flower design on the left (FL11). The tightness of the chain stitch for the outline of the design and the use of colors makes this a design with special impact.

Eldee chose to do only the outlines, while others may fill in every part of the design. There is no right or wrong way and each technique lends itself to its own interpretation, impact, contrast and creativity.

Blanch Jones has completed twelve African Folklore Embroidery designs. Her work is so meticulous and consistent with such careful thought and consideration given to color.

Taffy Stern completed design OC11, "Under the Sea", seen on the next page The use of beadwork

throughout this design makes it unique. Whether a single strand of beads used for the vein of the leaf or part of the rock, or individual beads stitched into the hair and clothes, the beadwork combined with the fine chain stitch make this a true work of art. Taffy used multicolored glass beads in a string formation for the center of the design.

Both seahorses are infused with yellow beads and the crustacean's pink shell has pink beads. The red chain stitch used for the outline of the starfish emphasizes the red beads inside. Thin elongated green beads form the shell of the turtle and then green thread Cabbage (30) accentuates the green in the beads. Taffy outlined the stingray in variegated Lavender (34) with chain stitch. This is really an example of outstanding beadwork and bead incorporation into an African Folklore Embroidery design.

My exceptionally talented and vivacious aunt, Patricia Flaum, in Johannesburg, completed this African Folklore Embroidery tablecloth.

Carol Fitzhugh, Colorado

Each of Carol's designs are works of art, from her choice of color to the consistency of her stitches.

Bettiray Willis embroidered design AF24 and then stitched it onto the back of a denim jacket

This is the back of Carole Ireland who after embroidering her bird with attitude (B15) turned it into a wearable art vest.

Monique Smallson completed design AF15 and then turned it into a purse

Ann Cheek La Rose completed her design, "African Village," in 2006. Using design AF21 as the center block she did a log cabin pattern using genuine African fabrics from Ghana and prints from Senegal; traditional cowry shells, African trade beads, and metal buttons (to symbolize a gold weight) were added for interest.

Terri Wharburton converted the flower design (FL19) on the right into a pillow using green fabric for the border.

Ginny Davis, Colorado, embroidered each of these designs and then stitched them into a quilt.

There are a total of ten embroidery designs within this quilt. Ginny used two of the basic kit designs—AF25 and ostrich design (B21) —as well as two super kit, 17-inch square designs,

The Mask (AF27) and The Big Five (AN16), and then several 8-inch designs—Rhino, Lizard, Bird, Lion, Snake and Chameleon.

My Favorite Places to Visit in South Africa

I have so many places that I love to visit while in South Africa, so I have listed a few of them. Time spent in the places below inspired many of the designs.

CAPE TOWN, WESTERN CAPE

Boulders Beach: Thousands of penguins have made their home on Boulders Beach. The moms make their nests on the beach and the babies are born there. The penguins coexist with people who come to swim, sunbathe and relax. These penguins are not afraid or inhibited by humans. My son often swims in the ocean with them a few feet away. www.go2africa.com/south-africa/cape-town/african-safari-guide/boulders-beach

Butterfly World: www.places.co.za/html/butterflyworld.html

Cape Point: Where the waters of the Atlantic and Indian Ocean meet. View up close and very personal monkeys, guerillas and baboons. There is also a wide selection of bird and flower life. www.capepoint.co.za

Chapman's Peak: The most magnificent view of the Indian Ocean meeting with the Atlantic Ocean. You can expect to see monkeys who have made their home here; they may climb on top of your car. www.chapmanspeakdrive.co.za

Greenmarket Square: African artifacts on sale. www.greenmarketsquare.com

Kirstenbosch Botanical Gardens: The flowers at Kirstenbosch provided the inspiration for many of the floral designs. Home to many bird species (including breeding owls, guinea fowl and sugarbirds), and small endemic mammals (Cape Fox, small grey mongoose and Cape Otter), it is definitely worth a visit and one of my favorite places. www.sanbi.org/frames/kirstfram.htm

Monkeyland Primate Sanctuary, Plettenberg Bay: www.monkeyland.co.za

Ostrich Farms, Oudtshoorn: www.safariostrich.co.za

Robben Island Museum: Originally known as Seal Island and currently home to an abundance of penguins, tortoises, birds and sea mammals. Nelson Mandela, the first democratically elected president of South Africa, was a prisoner on Robben Island for twenty-seven years. In 2001, Nelson Mandela officially opened the Nelson Mandela Gateway to Robben Island. Today Robben Island is seen as a symbol of the triumph of the human spirit. A tour of Robben Island includes a ferry trip to the island, a guided tour of the prison by an ex-political prisoner who spent time as a prisoner on Robben Island, as well as a bus tour of the island's historic buildings and indigenous flora and fauna. www.robben-island.org.za

Table Mountain: www.tourismcapetown.co.za

The Garden Route: www.gartour.co.za

Victoria & Alfred (V&A) Waterfront: This is a working harbor offering everything from historical sites to upmarket shopping malls, arts and crafts markets, theaters, live music and entertainment. The history of the V&A Waterfront dates back to 1860, when Prince Alfred, Queen Victoria's second son, tipped the first rock for construction on Cape Town's original breakwater. The original Alfred basin could not handle the increased shipping volumes brought by the advent of steam, and subsequently a larger basin, the Victoria Basin, was built. In 1988 the Victoria & Alfred Waterfront Company was given the mandate to develop the historic harbor basins to combine tourism and commerce, with the continuing operation of the working harbor. www.places.co.za/html/va_waterfront.html

World of Birds: Is the largest bird park in Africa and one of the very few large bird parks in the world. www.worldofbirds.org.za

DURBAN, KWAZULU-NATAL

African Art Centre: Located in Durban, this non-profit art center provides an outlet for creative cultural works, and promotes traditional artistic work of local artists, providing artisans with income. This art gallery promotes and sells original works of art, sculpture, beadwork, tapestries, rugs, ceramics and carvings from the Zulu and Xhosa traditions. www.places.co.za/html/artcentre.html

Mitchell Botanical Gardens: A beautiful botanical gardens with peacocks and other birds.

San Lameer: This is one of my favorite places in the world; my in-laws first introduced me to this beautiful place twenty years ago. It has such wonderful memories for my husband and I. Located on Durban's South coast, it is a haven for birds, monkeys and other wildlife such as buck, deer and zebra. www.sanlameer.co.za

Ukhahlamba Drakensberg Mountains: www.kzn.org.za/kzn or www.kznwildlife.com

http://1000hills.kzn.org.za/1000hills/index.html

JOHANNESBURG, GAUTENG

Apartheid Museum: Located in Ormonde near Gold Reef City. www.apartheidmuseum.org

Bruma Craft Market: Features African art on display and available to purchase. www.wheretostay.co.za/information/topic/656

Croc City Crocodile Farm: Croc City crocodile farm provides the opportunity for the public to observe one of the world's most spectacular predators at close range. Croc City Crocodile Farm is situated north of Johannesburg, close to game parks, Lanseria International Airport, the Cradle of Humankind and en route to Hartebeespoort Dam. The area is called Nietgedacht and falls within the Crocodile Ramble area.

www.sa-venues.com/attractionsga/croc-city-johannesburg.htm

Discovery of Gold and Soweto Day Trips: www.gauteng.net

GAME RESERVES

The Kruger Park www.krugerpark.co.za

Pilanesberg Game Reserve http://pilanesberggamereserve.com/index.html

Kwa Maritane Game Reserve www.legacyhotels.co.za

Bakubung Game Reserve www.legacyhotels.co.za

Old Reef City: Tour gold mines and learn how gold was discovered in South Africa. www.goldreefcity.co.za

Lesedi Cultural Village: located an hour outside of Johannesburg. Here you will encounter different tribes and learn about their cultures and traditions. www.lesedi.com

Ndebele Cultural Village: Located at Zebra Country Lodge in Pretoria. +27-12-470-5300

Rosebank Flea Market: Features African art on display and available to purchase. www.wheretostay.co.za/information/topic/657

NAMAQUALAND, NORTHERN CAPE

Namaqualand: www.northerncape.org.za

Other tourism websites:

www.cybercapetown.com and www.go2africa.com

Interested in learning more about AIDS in South Africa and how you can help?

www.starfishcharity.org , www.kidzpositive.org and www.one2onekids.org

My Mom Barbara's Favorite South African Recipes

Hot Milk Sponge Cake

My mom used to bake this cake for the weekend.

Ingredients	Directions
4 extra large eggs 1½ cups sugar 1 tsp vanilla essence 4 tsp baking powder 125 grams butter or margarine (¼ stick) 1 cup milk 2 cups flour	Beat eggs for 5 minutes till smooth and frothy. Add vanilla to sugar and beat for 5 minutes. Sift flour three times. Add flour to sugar. Add milk and butter to flour and sugar mixture and blend with wooden spoon. Add baking powder. Add eggs. Mix together. Put in oven at 350 degrees for 20 minutes.

Hot Asparagus Crisp Tart

This we usually had as a starter or appetizer though you can also serve it as a side dish.

2 tins canned asparagus

3 tbsp butter or margarine

4 tbsp flour

½ cup milk

½ cup grated cheese

Pinch of salt

Place asparagus in dish. Pour the juice from the asparagus tin into a heated frying pan, mix in butter. When the butter has melted add in flour one spoon at a time. While stirring, add in milk and salt. Pour mixture over asparagus, sprinkle with grated cheese, and place in oven at 350 degrees for 45 minutes.

Barbara's Famous Apricot Jam Biscuits

The first thing I want to eat when I get back to South Africa are these delicious biscuits my mom makes.

2 cups flour

1 tsp baking powder

8 tsp sugar

500g or 1lb butter or margarine

2 large eggs

1 tsp vanilla essence

Apricot jam

Cream butter and sugar, add eggs and vanilla essence, add in flour and blend and knead dough. Dough must not be too hard. Divide dough in half. Put one half in freezer and the other half spread out over a baking sheet. Spread apricot jam on top, take out dough from freezer and grate it over the jam. Place in oven at 350 degrees and bake for 30 minutes.

Hot Potato Pudding Dessert

Ingredients	Directions
3 cups grated, rinsed potatoes 3 tbsp grated onions 4 tbsp butter or margarine 3 eggs, lightly beaten Pinch of salt ½ cup flour 1 tsp baking powder	Mix all the ingredients together and place in a baking dish. Bake in the oven at 400 degrees until brown and crispy.

Peppermint Crisp Pudding

This was a dessert for very special occasions

Ingredients	Directions
Tin condensed milk	Line the bottom of a buttered dish with graham crackers. Boil the tin of condensed milk in hot water on the stove for 50 minutes. When condensed milk has turned to caramel take the tin out of the boiling water. Beat cream. Place caramel on top of the graham crackers, and cream on top of the caramel. Sprinkle with mint chocolate. Repeat the layering process. Place in fridge for an hour to cool and set.
Plain vanilla cookies or graham crackers	
Mint chocolate	
250ml cream	

Cottage Pie

Growing up this main dish was a frequent meal in our home.

Ingredients	Directions
1lb ground beef or turkey	Sauté meat and onion in a frying pan till golden brown. Add ketchup and mix. Boil potatoes; when soft, peel off skin and mash. Place cooked meat in dish. Spread mashed potatoes on top of the meat. Place in oven at 350 degrees for 45 minutes.
1 onion	
Five potatoes	
2 tbsp ketchup	
Pinch of salt	

My mom and I doing our favorite past time, African Folklore Embroidery and my dad and son Joshua in the background, doing woodwork, making a kennel for our new dog and nieces Shoshana and Aviva, getting their first introduction to bead art.

77

African Folklore Embroidery by my Mom, Barbara

Acknowledgements and Dedications

To my darling husband, Gary Roy, I love and admire you so much. Thank you for always encouraging me to pursue my dreams. Thank you for all your love and support. I love you VVVVVVVVV much. You are my rock! Thank you for always holding my hand throughout lifes journey, for all your help with the book and for making my dreams a reality.

My precious son, Joshua, you are my precious and special boy. I love you so much. Your dad and I are so lucky to have you as our son. You bring us so much love, happiness and joy. I love you up to the moon and back again.

To the most wonderful sister in the world, Michele Medved. I so appreciate your continued love, support, affection and encouragement. It is a dream come true to be able to share in each other's everyday lives.

To my parents, Abe and Barbara Barishman, for your unconditional love, ongoing support, enthusiasm and inspiration. For always being such excellent role models and imparting beautiful values and traditions. For fostering a love of learning and creating.

To my in-laws, Harold and Irma Raikin, I am very fortunate to be blessed with such wonderful in-laws who have always made me feel like their own daughter. Your advice to see the wood from the trees will always stay with me.

To my cousin, Lynette a.k.a. "my older sister," your creativity inspires me; you are a true woman of action and your support and enthusiasm is appreciated more than you can imagine.

To my very precious and dear friends, thank you so much for your ongoing encouragement for this book and for understanding just how important African Folklore Embroidery is to me.

To an incredible person and amazing friend, Stephanie Bien, thank you for taking so many of the photographs and your ongoing encouragement and support.

To my aunt, Patricia Flaum, whose boundless energy, creativity, enthusiasm and positive attitude are an ongoing source of inspiration.

To my sister-in-law, Raymonde Barishman, I love how the threads and embroidery have connected us and I am in awe of your beautiful needlework.

To my customers, many who have become friends over the past few years, thank you for your support.

To my loving brother, David, nieces, Lara, Shoshana, Aviva and Gila, and my nephew, Bradley, sister-in-law, Michelle, brother in law, Harry Medved, and Allan Gordon, and cousins, Caryn, Joey, Andrea, Izzy, Leon, Debbie, Cara and Samantha Boroda.

To the quilting industry and all the quilting, weaving and embroidery guilds who have been so welcoming to African Folklore Embroidery.

To girl scouts and troop leaders all over the US who have embraced African Folklore Embroidery and understand the importance of learning new skills and being exposed to other cultures.

To all African Folklore Embroidery educators in New Zealand, Canada and throughout the United States, thank you for spreading the passion, encouraging a love of stitching and interest in Africa.

To the talented women who allowed for their spectacular completed designs to be featured in their book, thank you so much, I am so impressed with how you have taken African Folklore Embroidery beyond the scope, tools and techniques of my classes.

To the girl scout troops and their troop leaders who have embraced African Folklore Embroidery and realize the importance of nurturing new skills and cultivating interest and enthusiasm in other cultures

To the African Folklore Embroidery educators throughout the United States , Canada , Germany , Spain and New Zealand , your creativity is an inspiration, thank you for your spreading the passion.

To the many talented women who submitted pictures (I wish I could have included them all, but keep sending me pictures of your design for my next book) of their completed designs for this book, a big thank you:

Robin Roberts (Table of contents page: peacock) , Pam Ross (Cover Page), Sharon Camping, Heidi Monaly, Analee Perica, Charlotta Jokinan , Jonda Fredel, Connie Anderson, Heather Ologue, Bonnie Vorpsan, Carol Chamblis, Barbara Barishman, Patricia Flaum, Lia Smith, Taffy Stern, Shirley Hanchett, Jeanette Wahl, Robbie Eben, Malka Dubowsky, Lynette Hasson, Blanche Jones, Ginny Davis, Sally Fastea, Una Nep, Chardel Blaine, Darlene Solotkin, Yvonne Eli, Jennifer Solotkin, Angie Polopsian, Lori Russel, Raya Kauffman, Elisa Purnell, Alexis Kjelstrom, Candy Hartman, Carol Fitzhugh, Carol Ireland, Eldee Norton, Monique Smallson, Terri Wharburton, Ann Cheek La Rose, Bettirae Willis, Joanne Bloemfield - You have taken African Folklore Embroidery to a whole new level!

Thank you Jessica Keet, editor and proof reader and Ruth M. Roth graphic design.

Biography — Leora Raikin

Leora Raikin, South African native, Business Science research graduate from the University of Cape Town and Los Angeles resident, has taught over 6,000 adults and children the art of African Folklore Embroidery.

She was taught this creative art by her mother. Leora's mission is to fuse art with education, promote a love and interest in needle arts, educate about life in South Africa, all through African Folklore Embroidery.

Leora and her African Folklore Embroidery educational programs have been written about in the Los Angeles Times, Fons & Porter's Love of Quilting, Daily News, Denver Post, Tacoma Weekly, LA Family, Needle Arts, Black Purl, SQE (Sewing, Quilting and Embroidery Professional), Bangor Daily News, Needlepoint Now,

Piecework, Pasadena Star, Acorn, Creative Leisure News, Quilters Path, CQMagonline for crazy quilters, Arizona Republic, Quilters Newsletter and Sublime Stitching. (Press articles at www.aflembroidery.com). She is featured on HGTV's DIY Channel show "Uncommon Threads" (Duct 254).

Leora has lectured, exhibited and taught workshops on African Folklore Embroidery throughout the United States at museums; public and private schools; quilting, embroidery and fiber art guilds; trade shows; camps; Girl Scout troops and private groups and organizations. With the increase in demand for lectures and workshops, The African Folklore Embroidery Educators Training Program was established to allow others to teach and share their knowledge on African Folklore Embroidery throughout the United States, Europe and North America.

Leora lives in Los Angeles, California, with her husband, Gary, son, Joshua, and Labrador, Pebbles.

Leora is a member of the Southern California Council of Quilt Guilds, NETA, National Embroidery Association of Teachers, Northern California Council of Quilt Guilds, Pomegranate Guild, the National Needlework Association, WAC, Wearable Art Connection, as well as several other local quilting guilds.

African Folklore Embroidery is affiliated with and supports Kidzpositive, www.kidzpositive.org, a South African AIDS charity in Cape Town.

Leora has lectured to the following guilds and quilting organizations:

- African American Quilters Guild, CA
- Amador Valley Quilt Guild, Northern CA
- Antelope Valley Quilt Guild
- Big Bear Quilt Guild
- Beach Cities Quilt Guild
- Camarillo Quilters Guild
- Chicago International Quilt Show
- Chula Vista Quilters Guild
- Coachella Valley Quilt Guild
- Conejos Valley Quilters Guild
- Embroidery Guild Association, Southern CA Chapter
- Empire, Manhattan Quilter Guild, New York
- Flying Geese Quilting Guild
- Fullerton Sample Guild
- Glendale Quilt Guild
- Houston International Quilt Show
- Santa Barbara Fiber Arts Guild
- Inland Empire Embroidery Guild
- Long Beach Embroidery Guild
- Los Angeles County Fair
- Los Angeles Embroidery Guild
- Minnesota Embroidery Guild Association
- Nipoma Quilt Guild
- Nite Owl Quilt Guild
- Orange County Quilt Guild
- Orange Grove Quilters Guild
- Quilters By the Sea Guild, Long Beach, CA
- Redlands Citrus Belt Quilt Guild
- Road to California, Ontario, CA on lecturing faculty 2006, 2007 & 2008, lectures &workshops
- Sacramento Embroidery Guild
- San Fernando Valley Quilt Guild
- Santa Clarita Quilting Guild
- Santa Monica Quilters Guild
- South Bay Quilters Guild
- Ventura Weaving and Fiber Art Guild
- Wearable Art Connection Guild

Leora has taught African Folklore Embroidery at the following schools:

- Anderson Enrichment
- Bais Rebbe Day School
- Bay Laurel
- Buckley School
- Chandler
- Chime Charter School
- Colfax
- Fairfield Middle School
- Heschel Day School
- Justice
- Kadima Day School
- Kester
- Lanai
- Los Encinos
- Multicultural Learning Center
- Nestle
- Pomelo
- Pressman Academy
- Scholastic Advantage
- Sinai Akiba
- Valley Beth Shalom
- View Point
- Westland Woodlake Elementary
- West Valley Christian

Leora has taught African Folklore Embroidery for the City of Los Angeles Parks and Recreation Board at the following recreation centers:

- Shadow Ranch Recreation Center
- Sherman Oaks Recreation Center
- Tarzana Recreation Center
- Victory-Vineland Recreation Center
- Brighton Gardens
- Camp Yeladim
- Culver City Adult Education
- JCC
- Mt. Carmel Senior Center
- Northridge
- North Valley Therapeutic
- San Fernando Valley Adult Day Care
- Shomrei Torah Sisterhood
- Temple Aliyah Sisterhood
- United Synagogue Youth
- Valley Village Adult Day Care
- Woodland Park Adult Day Care
- The Art academy

Leora has also taught African Folklore Embroidery at the following institutions:

- JB Unique Needlework
- Joanne's Fabric Store
- Mar Vista Education Center
- Pierce College
- Skirball Cultural Museum
- Weavers Needle & Frame
- Westside JCC
- West Valley JCC

It has been wonderful having you along on this
creative safari adventure. I hope you enjoyed your
time and learned a little about South Africa, its
culture and traditions.

I am not going to say goodbye,

but rather as they say in Zulu,

"Hamba kahle" (Go well).

African Folklore
Embroidery Patterns

For additional information visit
www.aflembroidery.com

AF-24 - B	**AF-25 - B**	**AF-26 - B**	**AF-21 - B**
AF-22 - B	**AF-23 - B**	**FL-18 - B**	**FL-19 - B** / **AN-12 - B** / **AN-15 - B**
AF-29 - B	**AN-25 - B**	**OC-10 - B**	**OC-11 - B** / **AN-11 - B** / **AN-13 - B**
AN-14 - B	**AN-10 - B**	**AN-30 - B**	**BI-11 - B** / **BI-12 - B** / **BI-10 - B**
BI-13 - B	**BI-14 - B**	**BI-15 - B**	**BI-19 - S** / **BI-20 - S** / **BI-17 - S**
AF-10 - S	**AF-11 - S**	**AF-14 - S**	**AF-19 - S** / **AF-15 - S** / **AF-27 - S**
BI-18 - S	**BI-16 - S**	**AN-17 - S**	**AN-20 - S** / **AN-16 - S**

B = Basic Kit
11" square

S = Super Kit
17" square

Q = Quilt Block
8" square

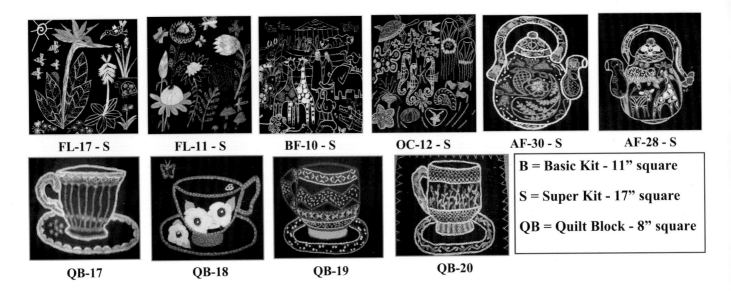

FL-17 - S	FL-11 - S	BF-10 - S	OC-12 - S	AF-30 - S	AF-28 - S

QB-17   QB-18   QB-19   QB-20

B = Basic Kit - 11" square

S = Super Kit - 17" square

QB = Quilt Block - 8" square

African Folklore Embroidery Variegated Embroidery Threads

All our exquisite threads are hand-dyed by House of Embroidery and are suitable for all types of embroidery ranging from hardanger to stump work and will magnificently enhance any design. We offer almost 100 colors in a variety of threads. For a complete color chart, visit www.aflembroidery.com

6-Strand Cotton Floss

Two complimentary colors per card - 5.4 yards each

Color-Fast / Washable / Light-Fast

Pearl 8 Cotton

Three complimentary colors per card - 9.7 yards each

Color-Fast / Washable / Light-Fast

Pearl 5 Cotton

Twisted - 24.2 yards per skein

Color-Fast / Washable / Light-Fast

Silk Thread and Ribbon

2mm & 4 mm Silk Ribbon - 3.25 yards per card

7mm Silk Ribbon - 2.2 yards per Card

Silk Thread - 33 yards per card

Color-Fast / Washable / Light-Fast